THE MIDLAND RAILWAY

A new history

ROY WILLIAMS

DAVID & CHARLES
Newton Abbot   London   North Pomfret (VT)

British Library Cataloguing in Publication Data
Williams, Roy
The Midland Railway : a new history.
1. Great Britain. Railway services : London,
Midland and Scottish Railway—to 1986
I. Title
385′.0941

ISBN 0–7153–8750–2

Photoset and printed in Great Britain by
Redwood Burn Limited, Trowbridge, Wiltshire
for David & Charles Publishers plc
Brunel House Newton Abbot Devon

Published in the United States of America
by David & Charles Inc
North Pomfret Vermont 05053 USA

CONTENTS

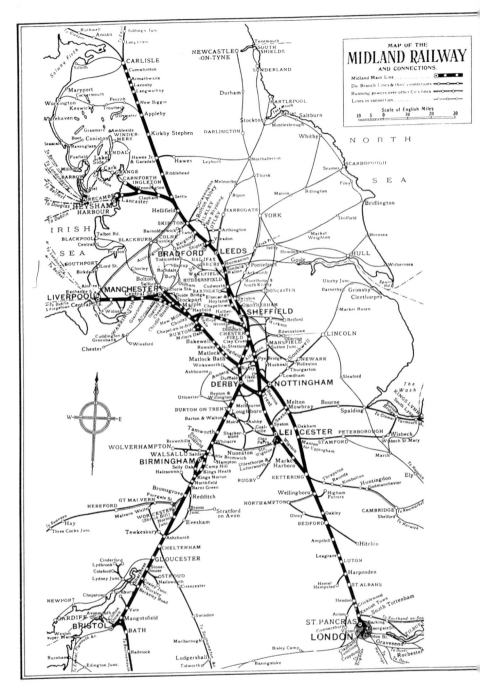

The Midland Railway published system map

1

THE BEGINNINGS

The Midlands Before the Railway

In the East Midlands of England lie three towns now grown to be great cities. Derby and Nottingham, only 14 miles apart, sit just to the south of the hills of the Peak District. Leicester is 25 miles further to the south over the ancient Charnwood Hills. Founded by the Danes, they were three of the five boroughs of the Danelaw. The other two, Stamford and Lincoln, did not grow as those which start our tale.

Our three towns were transformed by the invention of a country curate in the reign of the Queen Elizabeth. William Lee's restless mind invented the mechanical stocking frame, speeding twenty-fold the hand knitting of hosiery. Small enough to be used at home by one man, it started a major industry in the three towns; by 1770 there were 20,000 stocking frames in the East Midlands, used by poorly paid out-workers in their homes. Derby concentrated on fine silk, Nottingham on cotton, and Leicester on the coarser worsted. The life of the three towns came to depend almost entirely on stocking manufacture; the fast-flowing Derwent gave Derby the means to drive the machinery of an emerging engineering industry.

They were not by our standards large towns. Nottingham had 20,000 souls by 1820, Derby and Leicester rather more than half that number. The Midland Railway was to change them out of all recognition, to become the great cities that we know today.

To trace this story we must start with Leicester, where by 1820 the economic life of that town had remained unchanged since the coming of the worsted industry from London 100 years before. The town's main functions were just two in number—as a market place for the county's produce, and (more importantly) to manufacture worsted stockings and knitted goods for the rest of the world. Worsted was the key, for its spinning was best carried out in steam-driven mills instead

5

of by the old fragmented stocking frame industry, and steam engines required coal.

This came at first, expensively, from the coalfield near to Ashby-de-la-Zouch. After 1791 coal arrived at lower cost from the Mansfield area by the Trent and Soar Navigations. This left the pits to the east of the Ashby field without a market. The worsted industry was expanding rapidly, and all the Leicestershire coal owners could see was cheap Nottinghamshire coal arriving in their county town in ever-increasing quantities. Although the hilly region of Charnwood lay between them and the markets, a canal had been constructed as far as a tramway down to the Loughborough Navigation. Severe weather in 1799 destroyed a reservoir and damaged the embankments, leaving too high a cost for repair. This was the death-knell for a canal and tramway combination which never paid its way and which charged too much for transporting coal to give any advantage to the Leicester mill owners.

Founders of the Midland

(*top left*) John Ellis: This great Quaker – the father of the Leicester & Swannington – was the first Chairman of the Midland after Hudson's fall from grace. Originally a farmer from Leicester, he kept the line's fortunes free from financial malpractice during the Hudson years and rescued its fortunes in the lean years of the 1840s. *Leicester Art Galleries and Museums*

(*top right*) George Stephenson: Rightly called 'The Father of Railways', this self-taught engineer regarded the North Midland as his favourite line. During its construction he discovered coal measures near Clay Cross, founding his fortune. Stephenson retired within sight of the North Midland at Tapton Hall, occasionally lending a hand on the footplate of one of the 'long boiler' locomotives, built in Jarrow by his son, Robert. The Stephenson link motion – invented by the chief draughtsman – at Jarrow was first tried out on the NM. *Inst Mechanical Engineers*

(*bottom left*) George Hudson: This flawed genius, was responsible for the amalgamation forming the Midland. Called 'The Railway King', Hudson's railway empire stretched from Norfolk to Northumberland before his dubious financial dealings led to his disgrace. The Leeds & Bradford Railway, later part of the Midland, was the cause of his final undoing following a period of unparalleled influence in railway affairs, despite his cavalier financial management. Most of Hudson's railways still carry traffic. *National Railway Museum.*

(*bottom right*) Hudson Street, York: Once Lord Mayor of York, Hudson's fall from favour led to his memory being expunged from the streets of this ancient borough. Belatedly, his memory is enshrined in Hudson Street, near to the magnificent old NER station. This plaque is mounted on a wall of an inn called The Railway King. *Author.*

Canal Greed

So coal reached Leicester by one route only, and inevitably the cost was pushed up by the monopolistic canal owners. When the average weekly wage of a manual worker was around 20 shillings (£1.00) a week the cost of coal rose to 18 shillings (£0.90) a ton, of which ten shillings (£0.50) was for transport. To break this monopoly two Leicestershire men, more far-sighted than most, built one of the first railways in England, the Leicester & Swannington. Much of that noble line still remains, still bringing coal to Leicester.

The expanding population of Leicester was hungry for coal. Demand exceeded supply and prices rose, driven up by the combined monopoly of supplier and carrier, until the coal owner John Stenson and the quaker farmer John Ellis saw what was being achieved in the North by the new wonder steam-driven trains. A railway was proposed to tap the Charnwood Forest pits over towards Ashby, rivals to the Mansfield and Erewash Valley field; so started one of the very earliest railways in England. So started as well one of the greatest of English railways, the Midland, which had its earliest beginnings in the coal line over Charnwood.

Canal owners by their greed thus encouraged the development of the railways. Canals in the Midlands once the lifelines of industry are now scenic holiday haunts. Let us take a look at them first. Canals had a brief glorious summer in the 18th Century, feeding the Industrial Revolution, carrying coals and iron in the industrial heart of England. Many of the older railway engineers learned their trade on the canals. Indeed, the early construction workers were called 'navigators' from the great navigations they built on the Trent, the Mersey, and in the Black Country.

Canals near Leicester and Nottingham

The development of the very early railways in the Midlands was so intertwined with the canal systems of England that we need really to look at the complex of canals which fed coals, minerals and agricultural produce around the East Midlands in the 1800s. Lucidly described by Charles Hadfield in *Canals of the East Midlands*, they form a fascinating tale in themselves.

Before the Leicester & Swannington Railway was built, coals from the Erewash Valley pits and from those around Mansfield were taken down to Nottingham, further south to Leicester, and even down to

London, through the Erewash Canal, the Trent Navigation and the Loughborough and Leicester Navigations. Of these the Erewash and the Loughborough were the earliest, built under closely linked managements between 1876 and 1878.

The Loughborough enterprise used the River Soar as far as Bishop's Meadow until the river became too shallow for navigation, when a canal took over into Loughborough. The Navigation was an immediate success, paying a dividend of 20 per cent by 1790. John Smith, the engineer to the Loughborough Navigation, also surveyed the Erewash Valley Canal to tap the Nottinghamshire pits. Leaving the Trent at Sawley, near to the mouth of the Soar, the canal followed the west bank of the river to just above Ilkeston, changing to the east bank as far as Langley Mill, with a waggon way from the Mansfield pits meeting the canal at Pinxton.

Map of the Canal System between Nottingham and Leicester

Early Midland Days – The *Jenny Lind*: Bought by Kirtley from E. B. Wilson & Co of Leeds, these locomotives enabled the infant Midland to pull its ever-increasing traffic. They could show a fine turn of speed on light trains, and were later developed by Kirtley to his own designs, into even more reliable and light-footed locomotives. *L&GRP*.

One of the earliest photographs of any steam locomotive shows this Derby-built 2-2-2, built May 1853. Developed from the *Jenny Lind*, this locomotive was originally numbered 112. Even in the 1850s, Midland men were smartly dressed in a style of uniform which remained unchanged into the 20th Century. *L&GRP*.

In 1789 these waterways were transformed by the new Cromford Canal, with William Jessop as engineer. This line left the Erewash Canal at Langley Mill, following the Erewash Valley as far as Ironville, tunnelled under the hills by the 2,966 yd Butterley Tunnel to meet the River Amber, then turned up the Derwent Valley to Cromford.

The canal was wide enough for coal barges below the tunnel, but the tunnel and locks above it were narrow-boat territory only. Jessop, with his assistant Outram of early tramways fame, had to call on all their knowledge and experience in building the Cromford line. The canal was built through hilly country, not the flood plains of the Trent or the Soar. The long Butterley Tunnel, an aqueduct, and 14 locks in a length of just over 14 miles taxed the builders' experience and shareholders' pockets to their limits. The 'Cromford' was at the very heart of the Industrial Revolution, for it served the famous cotton mill built by Arkwright at Cromford, the first factory to work on a 24-hour basis and lit by new-fangled lamps. Its lights blazing out in the valley ushered in a new era of manufacturing. The canal allowed the formation in 1790 by Jessop and Outram of the Butterley Iron Company, one of the earliest great iron foundries outside Wales. The words 'Butterley Iron Company' which can still be seen in the great London terminus of the Midland tell of the partnership between the iron industry and the railway down the years.

Traffic and financial results of the Erewash canal were brilliant successes. Total traffic in 1802–3 at 154,775 tons, of which 75% was coal, increased to 320,571 tons by 1840–1, coal accounting for two-thirds of the total. Tolls at around nine pence (£0.04) per ton amounted to £5,780 in 1802–3, rising to £12,086 in 1840–1, for a line costing only £7,880. It is not surprising that dividends in 1840–1 were £24 per £100 share. Canals were moneyspinners there; the Erewash Canal dividends rose to an amazing 51% by 1815.

The Leicester line came later. In 1791, after a number of false starts, a Bill authorising the Leicester Navigation was passed. It encompassed two lines, one from Loughborough to the Charnwood Forest pits, important to the story of the L&S railway, the other into Leicester. William Jessop was the engineer, with young Christopher Staveley as assistant. The Leicester line was built easily, partly as a Canal and partly as a navigation to the Soar, at a cost of around £45,000.

The Leicester line also earned rich dividends for the company, taking coals to the rapidly expanding worsted mills of Leicester. Over 16% was paid in 1825, a good return by any standard. The line's monopoly led to the building of the Leicester & Swannington, and dividends fell when coals were taken from the Charnwood Forest pits by rail, down to 12½ per cent in 1840, and then lower still.

The story of the Charnwood branch is not so happy. This line was not built through good canal country; there was no flood plain to keep costs low, nor was there a river valley to use. Built across the hills of Charnwood, the combined tramroad and canal left the Loughborough Canal wharf by a tramroad for the two miles to Napantan, followed by a canal to Thringstone Bridge, near to Swannington in the Charnwood coalfield. The first tramway to use fishbellied rails, the line was at last operational in 1797. Trade was poor as the Leicestershire coal owners could sell their product more readily in Birmingham via the Ashby Canal. The price of Coleorton coal at Napantan was nearly 10 shillings (£0.50) per ton with transport to Leicester still to pay, so Charnwood coal cost in the region of £1.00 per ton in Leicester when Nottingham coal was selling at 18 shillings (£0.90) per ton.

Then in 1799 disaster struck. At the thaw after a heavy snow a new reservoir burst, causing damage to housing and farmland. An aqueduct was destroyed and an embankment damaged. Jessop estimated £6,193 for repairs and compensation. Even though the line was open again by the end of 1801, no-one wanted to use it. It never really competed with the canal route down from the Erewash Valley and it closed, Leicester coal coming from Nottingham, and from Nottingham only. Rates went up, coal became expensive in Leicester—and John Ellis had heard from his Quaker friends in the North about the new, successful railways. A man of courage and sagacity, aided by a coal owner Stenson, he decided on a railway for Leicester coal. The Leicester & Swannington Railway was born.

The Leicester & Swannington Railway

The story goes that John Ellis (who knew George Stephenson, then building the Liverpool & Manchester Railway) travelled to see the great engineer when he was engaged on the difficult task of crossing the great bog of Chat Moss. Stephenson was persuaded, despite his preoccupations, to take an interest in a line of railway to run from Leicester to the coalfield near Ashby-de-la-Zouch. He could not undertake the survey himself, owing to his commitments on the Liverpool line. He did however recommend his son Robert, who had just returned from South America, to survey the line under the elder Stephenson's guarantee.

12

With Thomas Miles as joint surveyor, a route 16 miles, 5 chains long was proposed. Starting at the West Bridge over the River Soar at Leicester, it headed northwards along the Soar Valley for over a mile to pass through the straight and level Glenfield tunnel (1,796yd) to the valley of the small River Rothley. The line then ran beside the river as far as Desford, about five miles west of Leicester, swinging after Desford in a north-westerly direction towards Bagworth. Gradients were slight until Bagworth, where the surveyors laid out a self-acting 1 in 29 inclined plane. After the summit (565ft) at Saunton Road, the line was passed through a cutting at Battleflat before reaching Swannington by means of a further inclined plane, at 1 in 17 steeper than that at Bagworth. As this plane ran down towards the coal pits, a stationary engine was needed to pull waggons to its summit. The estimated cost of the railway, complete with three branches to pits and 'with all necessary equipments' was £75,450. The track was to be single throughout. The sum of £58,250 was raised at the first meeting to discuss the line, held at The Bell Inn, Leicester, on 12 February 1829. A further sum was raised by George Stephenson from Liverpool interests, bringing the total capital to £90,000. The company's first Act, with some unusual features, was obtained on 29 May 1830. Tables of tolls were to be posted at gates with the collectors' names attached. More commonly, the gauge was 4ft 8in, and the widely ignored clause was inserted requiring that engines should consume their own smoke.

It is difficult to appreciate at this time, when railways are a mature and well tried form of transport, the magnitude of this undertaking. Although but a single line 16 miles long, it was only the fifth line to be authorised in England and was opened six years before Birmingham was connected to London by rail. The Glenfield Tunnel was by any standard a major undertaking, and in 1830 called for great courage on the part of the engineer and the proprietors. It is small wonder that the overall estimates were well short of the final costs of the completed line.

Staking-out the line started quickly. Construction started in September/October 1830. In common with many early railways, inexperienced contractors soon ran into difficulties; two had ceased operation by March of the next year. The major headaches lay in the construction of the tunnel, which was a very substantial and novel undertaking for the times. The trial borings had led to the belief that the tunnel would be driven through stone, not therefore needing a lining. In the event 500yd was through sandstone, which needed a brick lining to a depth of 14in to 18in. This doubled the cost of the tunnel over that estimated. Matters were complicated by the accidental death of the contractor responsible for the tunnel. His partners had to be released from part of their contract which was re-let, and 18 months were to pass before the tunnel was finished. So novel was the railway that the engineer had to put gates at each tunnel entrance to keep out sightseers!

After much impatient worrying by the shareholders the line was at last opened with a triumphal train in July 1832. The occasion was somewhat marred when the locomotive *Comet* lost its chimney at the entrance to Glenfield Tunnel, because as it happened the track had been packed-up for a few fateful yards. Passengers on the inaugural train had to wash off the soot in the nearby brook.

Completion of the upper part to Swannington was not achieved until October, due mainly to difficulties at the long cutting at Battleflat. One year and one resident engineer later, the whole line into Swannington was opened in August 1833. The pioneering line, the first in the Midlands, was a great success, bringing the price of coal in Leicester down to 11 shillings (£0.55) a ton from 18 shillings (£0.90). Its beneficial effects were both immediate and far reaching; several collieries previously closed due to the high cost of transport were opened again. Stone quarries near to Leicester were expanded to meet the demand for buildings in the growing towns. Whole new towns, one rejoicing in the descriptive name of Coalville, were built as a direct result of the new railway. Most important of all, the courage and foresight of William Stenson and John Ellis pointed the way to a major revolution in industry and transport throughout the middle of England.

This very early line had no textbook of railway construction to follow—it made up the rules as it went along, as for example in the matter of stations. We now take it for granted that railways have stations for the convenience of passengers. Not so on the Leicester & Swannington. Passengers were not really encouraged anyway, so they just followed the happy coaching habit of using inns near the (ungated) road crossings. At one of these, the Stag and Castle near to Thornton, legend has it that the locomotive whistle was invented! The locomotive *Samson* hit a loaded horse-drawn cart, causing distress to all but the undamaged locomotive. It is said that Stephenson the elder went to see a musical-instrument maker in Leicester, and between them they devised the first steam whistle. Sadly no documents exist to give credence to this well-loved legend. Inns were also used at two other places including the Long Lane crossing, now the town of

Coalville, but beyond that inn there was no passenger accommodation to the end of the line.

The railway only had ten locomotives, eight or fewer of which were in service at any one time. They were on the whole under-powered. The first locomotive, *Comet*, was shipped from Robert Stephenson & Co in 1832. *Phoenix*, *Samson*, and *Goliath* were also bought from the same firm, the last two being converted to 0-4-2s by the addition of wheels sent from Newcastle soon after they were tested. A similar 0-4-2, *Hercules*, was ordered in mid-1833, also from Newcastle.

By the autumn of 1833 it was evident that the locomotive stock was too small and generally underpowered. A six-coupled locomotive, one of the first to be supplied in the country, was obtained from the Stephenson Company.

By 1834 the Liverpool members of the board were pressing for locomotive orders to go to the North-West. The result was the purchase of *Vulcan* from Tayleur's as well as two locomotives from Haigh's. By a happy thought the early locomotives are all remembered in the names of streets in Leicester near to Glenfield Tunnel.

The best-known feature of the line has always been the Swannington Incline and its stationary engine. The incline ran down towards the mines, so coal had to be hauled up a 1 in 17 slope towards Leicester by the single-cylinder stationary engine, one of the earliest to use piston valves. The engine, which is now preserved in the National Railway Museum at York, had a long and uneventful life, largely undisturbed by work.

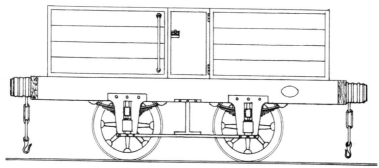

LEICESTER & SWANNINGTON R^Y
OPEN PASSENGER CARRIAGE ~
Completed ~ June, 1832

Leicester & Swannington Railway lower class carriage

The Leicester & Swannington Today

It is good to note that this line is still in use, 150 years after its opening. The Leicester end was diverted in 1849 to join the Midland main line just south of the main Leicester station, then at Campbell Street, skirting to the south of the town centre to avoid the expensive inner area. The Midland also extended the line at the Swannington end to form a through route still used between Leicester and Burton-on-Trent.

Apart from the section into West Bridge closed in 1966, coal and goods still pass along its single track. The L&S is held in great affection by the citizens of Leicester and rightly so. It was a real pioneer in the world of railways. Its building involved the solution of engineering problems of great magnitude for the times, while it gave a first-class coal and goods service to its area, building up a coalfield which still thrives. Leicester has commemorated the line in any number of ways. The Bosworth public house near the old demolished West Bridge terminus has a lively accurate mural on its wall. A second mural has been painted at the junction of Fosse Lane (and appropriately) Stephenson Road. The observant will also notice that the locomotive painted at the entrance to the small nature park near to West Bridge is the *Comet*.

Notts Fights Back

On the morning of 16 August 1832, one month after the opening of the Leicester & Swannington as far as Bagworth, a group of Nottinghamshire coal owners met at the Sun Inn at Eastwood to discuss a crisis in their affairs. They met weekly and usually their gatherings were routine, but this week things were very different. The Leicester market had been taken from them by the new railway across Charnwood to the Ashby pits.

Since the opening of the Soar navigation in 1791 coal from the Erewash Valley and the Mansfield area had travelled down the Cromford Canal, the Trent, the Loughborough Canal and the Soar Navigation to the booming town of Leicester. The two monopolies, coal-owners and canal operators, did very nicely out of this market, selling coal at close on twenty shillings (£1.00) a ton. Since the coming of the L&S had completely undermined this trade, the coal owners at first invited the canal proprietors to lower their charges by three shillings and sixpence (£0.17½) a ton. This they declined to do. The determined coal owners first threatened and then took the bold step of proposing to convert an old well established waggonway, the Pinxton tramway, into a railway from the Erewash Valley to Derby and to Leicester. Acting quickly and decisively the coal owners, anxious to preserve their trade, resolved to call for subscriptions for the new railway. Thus was born the Midland Counties Railway. Later this line combined with others to make the Midland Railway—it can be said rightly that the Midland was conceived at that far reaching meeting of coal owners at the Sun Inn, Eastwood, in 1832.

The birth of the infant Midland Counties Railway was hard, and two years were to follow before the necessary Act of Parliament was passed. In the beginning all went well; money came in from local investors, mainly coal owners. They were delighted to see the rich subscribers from Liverpool and Manchester, but their joy was short-lived as the powerful northerners saw beyond the small coal line into Leicestershire. Their objective was a railway to Rugby to join the shortly-to-be-completed London & Birmingham Railway, and hence to the massive London markets.

The local men had hired William Jessop to survey a line just as far as Leicester; the Manchester interest insisted on Rennie surveying a new route right down to Rugby, delaying all. By the summer of 1835, two years after the meeting at the Sun in Eastwood no progress had been made. Nevertheless protagonists of the line persisted, and on the suggestion of the Liverpool party among the shareholders a third engineer, Charles Vignoles, who had worked under Stephenson on the Liverpool & Manchester Railway was called in 'to find out the very best line to join the London to Birmingham Railway'. Vignoles changed the earlier estimates somewhat and increased the estimated cost from £600,000 to £800,000, even though the new route would have only one short tunnel under the Red Hill near the Trent.

The 'Vignoles Line' was approved by the board of the newly-constituted Midland Counties Railway despite a strong lobby by a group of railway promoters from Northampton, a major centre of leather goods manufacture which been by-passed by the London & Birmingham Railway some two years previously. Some railway historians hold to the view that Northampton discouraged the new railways; others are convinced that Robert Stephenson deliberately avoided a costly diversion to the town. In any event, the Midland Counties board was not persuaded to go via Northampton instead of Rugby.

Of the proposed capital of £1,000,000, one-third came from the Manchester area and the antics of the wealthy northern subscribers led to events that would do justice to any television drama. After safe passage through the House of Commons, the Midland Counties Railway Bill was delayed in the Upper House by the canal owners. The canal interests, fighting a rearguard action against the MCR, seized on an unlikely ally—no less than George Stephenson. Old George was surveying a railway to be called the North Midland, running from Derby north to Leeds. His surveyed line went near to the Erewash Valley Portion of the MCR route for several miles, and could take much valuable traffic from George's line. Parliament was very unsure of these new-fangled railways. Many members disliked any railway, but two for one small valley was just too much for them. One was more than enough. Meetings were held in smoke-filled committee rooms in the House and in the offices of the consulting engineers just round the corner near to Westminster Abbey. The Manchester party said to the MCR directors 'build only south from Derby—forget the Erewash Valley, the opposition is too strong, we will never over turn old George's lines.' So the MCR got its Act in June 1836, but the Erewash Valley portion—the start of the whole idea—was left out.

The Midland Counties Railway

The line as approved ran from Derby to Leicester by way of Long Eaton (later Trent Junction), Loughborough, and Syston, passing beyond Leicester through the villages of Wigston, Broughton and Ullesthorpe before joining the London & Birmingham line at Rugby. Rugby become a great railway junction, but astonishingly the major town of Nottingham was at the end of a track from the main line at Long Eaton. By the end of 1837 the whole line was under construction, the easy section between Derby and Nottingham lying along the Trent Valley being the first completed. By June 1838 the contracts were let for the permanent way, (standard gauge iron rails of 77lb/yd on stone blocks) and for those locomotives which would be needed for the opening of the Derby to Nottingham section. Work on this section was easy. Only one place near Derby where the Nottingham Canal was diverted tested the skills of the contractors. Here the cost of closing the canal for a diversion was set at £2 an hour by the hostile canal owners. Luckily a drought made the canal un-navigable at the very time the contractor wanted access and smart working saved him the cost of stopping canal traffic. The classical style Nottingham terminus was in keeping with the best of the stations built in England at that time. An entrance hall with two wings led to a passenger shed

covered with a light iron roof supported by a pair of arches. One wing
of the entrance building held the first and second class booking office,
the other was used by railway offices. Third class passengers had to
buy their tickets at a counter in the entrance hall!

The line to Leicester and to Rugby was opened in the summer of
1840, the main works being the two river crossings, one over the
Trent and the other over the Avon near Rugby. Kyanized larch
sleepers were used for the Trent junction to Rugby portion, while as
mentioned earlier the rails were held on stone blocks between Derby
and Nottingham.

The Midland Counties was built within its budget at £20,000 a mile
and was at first a financial success, paying a dividend of four per cent.
The service was by modern standards very sparse, only six trains a day
from Derby to Rugby and six back. The fast trains took 2¼ hours for
the journey, with onward connections to London, allowing 6¼ hours
for the whole journey. It took longer in practice, as connections at
Rugby were seldom made.

A New Industry Is Born

The Midland Counties in its short life helped in no small measure to
create one of the world's major industries, tourism. How this line,
designed mainly to carry iron and coal, came to start such a revolution
in leisure is a remarkable story. A wood turner in Market Harborough
near Leicester, Thomas Cook, earned his living at a wood lathe but
spent his spare time as a powerful Baptist preacher, greatly concerned
about the alcoholism rampant in the early 19th Century. A man of
considerable organising ability, he was asked to plan an open-air
temperance rally in the grounds of a large house close to
Loughborough.

He had heard of an excursion train run a few months before by the
Midland Counties and recognising that the rally would attract a much
larger following if people from Leicester could attend, he approached
the railway about an excursion from Leicester to Loughborough on
the day of the rally. The railway management agreed, and at Cook's
suggestion set a special fare of one shilling (£0.05) for the 24-mile
round trip, half that of the 'Parliamentary' fare of one penny a mile.
570 people took the special train, making it a huge commercial
success, while the successful rally attracted many more than would
have come from the small town of Loughborough.

Cook saw the value of these excursions to give the people of the fast growing and crowded new industrial towns a chance to escape from their surroundings. His new business flourished, coming of age at the time of the Great Exhibition of 1851, when Cook's excursions allowed thousands of working people from the Midlands and the North to visit London and the Exhibition.

Now, almost 150 years after the first Cook's excursion, Thomas Cook & Son is a byword for efficient travel, smoothly arranged. The company has offices in most major cities throughout the world where either the business traveller or the tourist can find help and efficient service.

The North Midland

While the projectors of the Midland Counties were fighting their battles in Parliament, the merchants of Leeds were becoming determined to secure the advantages of rail connection with the South and the rich London markets. Manchester was prospering from the Liverpool rail link—the canny Yorkshiremen were not going to be outdone by the cotton spinners over the Pennines. George Stephenson, living near Derby, at Ashby-de-la-Zouch, busy looking after his coal interests, was persuaded to survey a route south from Leeds to join the projected Midland Counties at Derby. This line was to become the North Midland Railway.

Every town with a far-sighted leadership wanted rail connection. York certainly had a leader in the up-and-coming George Hudson, of whom we will hear much. The future 'railway King' spearheaded plans for a line from York to join the projected North Midland at Normanton, a few miles south of Leeds. So we see how gradually the network of lines from the North of England was unfurling, Leeds and York to Derby, Derby to Rugby, and then by the London & Birmingham Railway to the great goal, the London markets.

Stephenson's route for the North Midland Railway graphically illustrates the differing ways in which these infant railways were being planned. In the planning of the North Midland we see laid out before us all the thinking of the early railway engineers—how they chose a line, which towns to serve, which to by-pass, and above all how to keep costs within reasonable sight of the money available.

Their hands were tied by the power of the puny locomotives of the 1840s. These could only just manage a gradient of 1 in 300 with full steam! The earliest railways like the Stockton & Darlington and the L&B were designed like canals, level stretches connected at different levels by rope haulage up inclined planes. By the 1830s such methods

20

could not cope with the vastly increased traffic, so the surveyors had to allow modest gradients even in the hilly northern industrial regions. The engineers favoured two differing ideas; one camp led by Stephenson, said 'build along valleys and put intermediate towns on branches.' The other camp led by his great pupil Locke, held to the view 'build in straight lines and dig deep cuttings to keep a level line'.

When planning the Derby to Leeds line, two routes were possible. One went via Sheffield, a major industrial town in a steeply-sided valley, guarded by the hills which fed the fast-flowing streams that powered the town's mills and forges. The favourite followed the valleys passing through Rotherham, an ancient monastic settlement to the north-east of Sheffield. What is more, this route by-passed the county town of Wakefield and the coal mines of Barnsley, but apart from one tunnel the line avoided major works and followed the low ground. The citizens of Sheffield, by then an important steel town, were not amused by the adoption of the 'valleys' route via Rotherham.

The line prepared for Parliamentary approval left Derby along the Derwent as far as Ambergate, where it turned to run beside the Amber for seven miles, crossing into the valley of the Rother by the great Clay Cross Tunnel. Chesterfield was skirted, but the hilly environs of Sheffield were completely avoided, the chosen route passing five miles to the east near to Rotherham, then a small village, now grown, thanks to the railway, to the size of Sheffield. Several large towns were ignored on the 40 or so remaining miles to Leeds, including Barnsley and Wakefield, with stations named for them miles away to the east. Vignoles was retained by Sheffield interests to oppose this route in Parliament, proposing instead a line up the Erewash Valley and then passing through Sheffield. After lengthy discussions in Committee the prestige of the Stephensons won the day in the House and the North Midland Act was passed on 4 July 1836.

Sheffield was not ignored completely but was reduced to branch status by the nominally independent Sheffield & Rotherham, now the focus of major industrial growth along the Don Valley. Before the line was built, Sheffield's industry was concentrated in the hilly parishes of the town centre; with the railway came huge iron and steel works along the flat water meadows of the Don. The whole stretch of line is now one massive steelworks, supplying the world's markets with high quality engineering steels.

Building the North Midland

The most difficult work on the route was boring Clay Cross Tunnel. Although not the longest tunnel driven in the late 1830s, Clay Cross was at a mile between portals long enough when every yard had to be won by the combined forces of navvy muscle and blasting powder. Construction was by the standard tunnelling method of the day. Ten shafts were sunk along the line of route. Tunnelling then started at each shaft bottom in both directions and at each tunnel end. The work was dangerous in the extreme; every bit of soil or rock was moved by hand in the dark, lit only by a few candles, with water always present. At Clay Cross coal measures were found, later developed by George Stephenson. The diggings were so wet that steam pumps at the top of the shafts worked night and day. The men became careless of the blasting powder used to move rock and accidents due to casual detonations were commonplace. In one fatality, the basket pulling the blaster up from the rock face got stuck in the shaft before the unfortunate navvy could reach safety. In other cases, whole barrels of powder were set off accidentally while men were smoking close by. At Clay Cross it is estimated that 11 men were killed, but no-one kept records.

After a tunnel was bored about 12ft into the rock, bricklayers moved in and lined the bore. Before the bricking of each section, falls of rock onto gangs of navvies were frequent and usually fatal. The work rate was prodigious; in one week a million tons of spoil were moved from 22 faces by gangs of around ten navvies, each man shifting 20 tons a day. The tunnelling lasted from February 1837 until August 1839, using 15 million locally made bricks set in a lining 18in thick, at a total cost of £105,460. The northern portal was so well built and designed that it is now a Grade II listed building.

All the early Midland lines were built without machinery by the muscle power of large bodies of specialised workers, who spent their lives moving to wherever railway construction was going on. The navigators were itinerant workers who worked and played hard. Much exploited by contractors, they built Britain's rail network by hand, and much of the continental rail system was also made by the British navvy, mile by weary mile. Given low wages by sub-contractors, they were further impoverished by the 'truck' system in which wages were paid in notes for shoddy goods, exchanged only at the contractors' shops, where they and their families were cheated shamelessly. Eventually Parliament passed the Truck Acts to stamp out this abuse. Navvies lived, usually out of wedlock, in hovels close to the workings and under appalling conditions; rioting and drunkenness were the frequent results. At Clay Cross a beerhouse owner owing money absconded, leaving some stock to be sold off. Navvies cheated by the man raided the store, and from the local account:

'several barrels of ale were immediately carried from the cellar to the room above; the ends were knocked out and a scene followed which is impossible to describe. The whole body of thirsty excavators rushed to the barrels armed with basins, kettles and cans and vessels of every conceivable description which they applied to their mouths and gulped down their contents and caused a scene of great drunkenness.'

The North Midland opened in 1840 and was Stephenson's favourite Railway—he bought a house near Chesterfield and settled down to look after the Clay Cross pits, discovered while boring the Tunnel. The North Midland, despite being planned as a valley line, still cost just over £36,000 a mile to build, nearly twice the estimated £20,689, and greatly in excess of the Midland Counties' £21,780 a mile, reflecting the cost of the Clay Cross Tunnel and cuttings at Oakenshaw and Normanton. These two railways also had very different attitudes to the design of stations, the North Midland having some of the best designed stations ever built. The civil engineer Francis Whishaw who described in detail all the lines of England in 1840, and who did not approve of generous provision for passengers, said of the North Midland stations:

'The stations of the North Midland Railway have afforded Mr Thompson the architect ample scope for the exercise of his talent, which is strikingly exhibited throughout the whole of the permanent buildings of this railway. But although highly estimating the elegantly chaste designs which characterise the architecture of the North Midland stations, we cannot but deplore the growing evil of expending large sums of money on railway appendages. Instead of cottage buildings, which for the traffic of most of the intermediate stopping places on this line would have been amply sufficient, we find the railway literally ornamented with so many beautiful villas, any one of which would grace the sloping lawn of some domain by nature highly favored.'

Francis Thompson was an enigmatic character who designed many railway stations in the 1840s. Thought to have been a London tailor with a flair for design, he created stations for the North Midland, the Chester & Holyhead, and the Eastern Counties Railways. His earliest work was for the North Midland. He used the Italian villa style for stations at Belper and Eckington, Tudor for those at Chesterfield and his masterpiece at Ambergate, perfectly symmetrical, like all his stations for this line. Ambergate was re-erected on a new site later. Fortunately we have a lithograph of the original station showing the beauty of its design. Pleasing to the platform prospect as well as that from the approach, it surpasses all but a few station designs ever built. The Northern terminus in the Leeds suburb of Hunslet was graced by a grand entrance topped by an arch exhibiting the arms of Leeds, Sheffield and Derby. What the citizens of Sheffield thought about theirs when the line only served the steel city with a branch is best left to the imagination.

The Birmingham & Derby Junction Railway

The builders of our early railways had to find answers to problems which were completely new to them. How, for example did one cope with competitive lines? Before the late 1830s railways were so far spread out that none competed with others for traffic. The Birmingham & Derby Junction Railway changed all that, facing competition from its earliest days. Conceived by Birmingham interests as a link to the Yorkshire industrial areas, it was built to tap the traffic which would come down the North Midland Railway through Derby to London, bringing it into direct competition with the Midland Counties Railway then being planned by the Nottinghamshire coal owners. When the two lines were opened they competed fiercely for London traffic, and it took a man of great but flawed commercial talents to resolve their conflict by the first railway amalgamation.

Going back to the gestation of the B&DJR, George Stephenson at the request of a Birmingham committee surveyed a line to Derby in 1835. The easily graded line would go from a station near the Curzon Street terminus of the L&B via Tamworth and Burton to Derby. A branch from Whitacre would run down to the L&B line at Hampton-in-Arden, with vital (and usually missed) connections to London.

The Act passed easily in the House of Commons, due to the active support of the Tamworth Member, Prime Minister Robert Peel, then at the height of his powers but even before the Act was passed the B&DJ and the MC fell out in a way worthy of a television drama. There were of course informal discussions between the boards of the three lines being planned in the Midlands in the 1830s and despite a certain coldness of feeling between the MC and the B&DJ boards, they agreed that if the Birmingham company withdrew its Hampton Branch, then the MC would drop from its Act the proposed line along the Erewash Valley to the Nottinghamshire coalfield.

When the Acts were published the Birmingham directors had honoured their agreement while the Midland Counties' had not. The B&DJ immediately put forward the Hampton branch line under the disguise of a nominally separate company. In the event the MC Pinxton branch was also dropped, but the Hampton branch went ahead!

The line was easy to build, following as it did the broad flat valley of the Trent from Derby as far as its junction with the Tame. Turning south, then west into Birmingham, there were no tunnels and few cuttings. Viaducts near Tamworth and near Alrewas carried the line over rivers. The directors were anxious to open the line ahead of the Midland Counties to gain as much London traffic as possible. In the event it opened on 5 August 1839, with public service starting a few days later. At this stage all traffic went via the Hampton branch, reversing there and going into the Curzon Street terminus of the L&B, taking two hours for the journey on one of three trains a day. Through coaches ran to and from Euston on one train a day in each direction.

The through route from the north of England was not completed for about a year, when a connection to the west of England in Gloucester was also opened. The opening dates of these independent but interconnected lines are:

North Midland (from Leeds)	1 July 1840
Birmingham & Gloucester (to the West)	11 December 1840
Midland Counties (to London via Rugby)	30 May 1839
Birmingham & Derby	12 August 1839

The B&G was only open to a temporary terminus at Camp Hill, so the traffic receipts of the B&DJ were lower than expected until through traffic from the North and to the West could flow. At the same time the Midland Counties was opened, taking traffic to London. The finances of the line were further aggravated by the tolls paid to the L&B for the Hampton to Birmingham portion of a journey from Derby, but this situation was relieved in 1840 when an independent line into Birmingham was authorised by Parliament. This was opened to a terminus at Lawley Street, near the new station of the Grand Junction and L&B lines on 9 February 1842, and the Hampton branch singled.

2

THREE YOUNG RAILWAYS

Introduction

By the end of 1850 there were some 6,000 miles of railway open for public traffic in Great Britain—in 1830 there had been under one hundred. These were the heroic years of railway building in this country, when all was new and unknown and no guidelines had been written for even the simplest operation. The three young railways meeting at Derby played a central part in these halcyon days, helping to set the pattern of railway working for years to come—even to modern times.

The engineers who planned and built the railways made surprisingly few errors as they went along, apart from a tendency to underestimate costs. After the contractors had departed ordinary mortals took over, facing the problems of daily railway operation with no background or experience. Recruited from all manner of occupations, but often from the armed forces or from the early police, the early railwaymen had to meet unforeseen problems on a scale never before encountered in business. The many facets of railway operation are diverse, stretching from recruitment, training and motivation of staff, to the assessment of fares and goods rates, proper keeping of time, safe regulation of traffic along the tracks before the telegraph, maintenance of locomotives, carriages and permanent way and so on through a thousand and one varied activities. Even a simple matter like time was complicated by the variation between 'London time' and the many country times. Staff uniforms had to be designed and bought, for the railwaymen were amongst the first civilians to wear them.

The men who managed the early lines were amateurs—the shareholders and directors—for the 'professional manager' was yet to appear. Local men of substance, they were entering business activities for which they had no training or prior knowledge, for there was none.

26

How the men of the 'Derby lines' managed is a lively and fascinating tale.

Two Great Stations: Curzon Street and Derby

The B&DJ line into Birmingham used a terminus specially built at Lawley Street, about one mile east of the city centre, just before the land starts to rise up towards the Bull Ring and the city markets area, sandwiched between the converging lines from London and the Grand Junction from the North. It was soon realised that this arrangement was unsatisfactory, as the station was about 40ft below the other two lines, with no direct connection. Locomotive sheds and repair shops were built at the site and the company's headquarters were transferred there in 1843. Goods traffic was transferred to the other lines by an incline to the Grand Junction, passengers having to walk about a quarter of a mile. This inconvenient arrangement lasted until 1851 when Lawley Street reverted to goods use, passenger trains going to the L&B terminus at Curzon Street, an outstanding building, which served the lines to Derby, Manchester, and London. Built in the classical style, it in turn fell to goods status when the New Street station of the London & North Western Railway was built in the 1880s to serve lines to London, the North, Derby and the West of England. Curzon Street fell into semi disrepair as a goods station and in 1980 was almost derelict. Then the Birmingham City Council acquired the building as a centre for urban renewal community projects. Now restored to its original glory, it is well worth an excursion into the Birmingham back streets to find and admire as one of the finest stations ever built.

With three lines coming together at Derby the question of joint station accommodation arose well before bitter arguments between the three companies started. First thoughts were for separate stations at a congested site called The Holmes between the River Derwent and the Derby Canal. Derby Council, which seemed to have a deal of common sense, withdrew its permission to build there, suggesting instead a site for a joint station to the south east of the town centre at a place known as Castle Fields.

The station, designed by the talented architect Francis Thompson, was NM property, with rent paid by the other two companies. The first joint station in the country, it had an imposing classical building serving only one low platform long enough for more than one train, with bays for the MC and the B&DJ trains at each end. An elegant iron roof covered a total of nine lines linked by small turntables. The station offices on the town side of the station included the NM board room, office accommodation, together with separate refreshment and waiting rooms for first and second class passengers. This station, copied later in other places, notably Huddersfield, was magnificent. Even the critical Whishaw says:

'The admirably contrived and elegant roofs, the spacious plat-forms, the great length of the whole erection, extending to upwards of a thousand feet. All unite in rendering it the most complete structure of the kind in the United Kingdom, or perhaps in the world.'

The original Thompson building was expanded as the railways grew. In the 1850s a third floor was added to the central block; later in 1872 a large *porte-cochère* was built to the front of the main entrance and a new board room added. By 1892 the railway was so well established at Derby that a magnificent frontage was erected for the figurehead provincial station of the line. Sadly it is all redeveloped now, despite valiant efforts by local conservation groups to preserve the original station buildings.

Francis Thompson also built a hotel to the south of the station, a radical innovation at the time making this elegant building the oldest railway hotel in the world! The charges are, however rather more than the original four shillings (£0.20) for a night's rest and three shillings (£0.15) for breakfast!

Another 'first' by the North Midland was a fine village of workers' cottages built for station clerks and porters at a time when Derby was dominated by slum dwellings. The Great Western Railway also built cottages at Swindon, but a little later than the North Midlands enterprise. These fine homes have now been beautifully restored and constitute an elegant conservation area in the centre of Derby.

The three companies also built their main locomotive depots at Derby. The NM shed was 16-sided, each side having a line radiating from a central turntable. Workshops for locomotive repairs were placed close by—at this early stage in railway development locomotives were nearly always bought from the independent makers, firms such as Robert Stephenson & Co, and Kitson of Leeds. These well founded shops would be the basis of the future great Derby locomotive works of the Midland Railway, destined to grow into one of the world's foremost railway workshops, and later to be the technical centre *par excellence* of British Rail, one of the foremost centres of railway engineering in the world. From such small beginnings arose the InterCity 125 units and the Advanced Passenger Train!

Locomotives of the Three Lines

Even while the three lines centred on Derby were being built railway locomotive design was changing and rapidly evolving. These lines started operation within a decade of the Rainhill trials on the Liverpool & Manchester Railway, when it was not even certain that locomotives should be used at all! There was no clear body of engineering opinion to guide the directors of the new companies towards the best suppliers or the most reliable design of locomotive. By the late 1830s three distinct schools of locomotive design had emerged from the wide assortment of types represented at the Rainhill trials. Some railways followed Stephenson's ideas, others preferred Bury's ideas, some Hackworth's.

Two of the three lines centred on Derby, the NM and the B&DJ chose the Stephenson model; the MC favoured Bury. Let us through the locomotive histories of these lines see which design came out on top. Robert Stephenson's firm had moved a long way during the 1830s from the *Rocket*, and by 1838 the Stephenson Company made a robust and workmanlike 2-2-2 locomotive derived from the *Planet*, with horizontal cylinders placed between massive outside rigid frames. In contrast, Bury & Co of Liverpool kept to a 2-2-0 design with bar frames, whose horizontal cylinders, like the Stephenson design, were placed between the frames.

Only six years after the Rainhill trials the Stephenson company had solved the basic problems of locomotive design. The *Patentee* was a remarkable achievement; its design was basically the same as the large 'flyers' used so well by Dariel Gooch for pace-setting express work a few years later on the Great Western Railway. Later designers added modified valve motions and a valve arrangement which allowed the steam to expand once inside the cylinder, but it can be fairly held that even the great Castles of the GWR arguably the best locomotives ever designed, owed their basic design to the *Patentee*.

In the 1830s Edward Bury, a former master builder, was experimenting with a different solution to the main problem which beset early locomotive designers—rail breakage. Cast-iron rails at only 35lb of metal to the yard were only able to support light locomotives, sprung as well as possible. Robert Stephenson used an extra pair of wheels to reduce the axle loads. Bury tried another way. He used a

Railway	Type	Wheel arrangement	Design	Number built
North Midland	Passenger	2-2-2	Stephenson	34
	Goods	0-4-2		10
		2-4-0		4
		0-6-0		1
Midland Counties	Passenger	2-2-0	Bury	37
		2-2-2		3
	Goods	0-4-0		6
		0-4-2		1
Birmingham & Derby Jct	Passenger	2-2-2	Stephenson	12
	Goods	0-4-2		2

2-2-0 wheel formation with bar frames instead of the heavy iron-wood sandwich frames of the Stephenson locomotives, giving lightness and springiness. Bury frames can be seen in the National Railway Museum in York on the locomotive *Lion* built for the Furness Railway. The bars of the frames are about 18in apart, with the upper one made of wrought iron of a rectangular section. The lower bar is round, for strength, except where the wheel horn blocks are attached to the bars—it is a rigid, light and well sprung construction.

The Bury locomotives also had a horizontal pair of cylinders inside the smokebox. A characteristic domed copper firebox cover topped a firebox D-shape in plan.

This successful design was used on the Midland Counties Railway and to some limited extent on other British lines, but it came into its own in North America. There, bar-framed locomotives were the norm until the 1900s. The design was well suited to the poorly laid tracks used to cover the vast distances of the USA and Canada at reasonable cost; the long, deep firebox was well adapted for burning bulky cottonwood. Although the Stephenson school of design won the day this side of the Atlantic, Bury won in North America. Bury's ideas put up a good fight in England, but the excellent English permanent way allowed the more ridged and reliable *Patentee* concept to flourish.

The directors of the North Midland and the Midland Counties had no experienced opinion to guide them; as in so many other things these three Derby lines were the first testing ground for rival new ideas and designs. The railways had to work it out for themselves, the Midland Counties Railway directors choosing Bury locomotives, as did those of the London & Birmingham. Not surprisingly, the North

Midland directors followed the lead of their engineer and chose the locomotives built by Stephenson & Co. In 1844 the 110 locomotives of the three lines were as shown opposite.

How did these designs compare? A typical Midland Counties bar-framed passenger locomotive had 5ft 6in driving wheels and two 13in × 18in inside cylinders. It weighed 12 tons 4cwt. Boiler pressure was 50lb/sq in, and the nominal tractive effort was just over 1500lb. The Bury locomotives have been criticised for their lack of strength and power but they lasted well, a group of eight with classical names, such as *Centaur* and *Siren* being withdrawn as late as 1855.

The typical Stephenson locomotive of the NM had 6ft 0in diameter driving wheels; with two 14in × 18in cylinders and 70lb/sq in steam pressure, the nominal tractive effort of these sturdy trend-setting locomotives was 2730lb at 65% boiler pressure. Similar locomotives built by other makers did not do so well; a number by Tayleur, Mather-Dixon, and others were broken-up in 1851, less than ten years old.

The twelve 2-2-2 locomotives of the B&DJ were of the *Patentee* type. Named after towns and rivers along the line, six of them built by Tayleur and by Mather-Dixon had twin domes. Three of the single-dome locomotives were very beautiful machines built by Sharp. Of equal interest was the locomotive superintendent of this short line, Matthew Kirtley. From the north–east, he had been a fireman on the Liverpool & Manchester Railway and had driven on the Leeds & Selby and on the London & Birmingham. Promoted from engine foreman at the small Hampton works of the line, he became at 28 its locomotive superintendent in 1841. We will hear much more about this remarkable man.

Carriages

All three lines had basically similar carriages, which were unbelievably stark, especially in third class. A picture from the Leicester Museum of Technology shows a Midland Counties train with first second and third class carriages. First class were 'stage coaches on a railway waggon' and would have been comfortable inside but unheated. All coaches were four-wheelers, with second class having sides but no windows; thirds were open waggons with low sides and no seats! Fares for journeys were not low; Nottingham to Derby on the Midland Counties Railway, quoted in the *Nottingham and Derby Railway Companion* cost three shillings and sixpence (£0.17½) first class, two shillings (£0.10) second class, and one shilling (£0.05) third class at a time when the weekly wage of a manual worker was around twenty-five shillings (£1.25). So the third class fare was around four per cent of an average weekly wage. Today this fare is only one per cent of the average weekly manual wage.

Signalling

These lines were a microcosm of the development of railway signalling, as in most other railway matters. Trains were not frequent, which helped! The only possible method of train control was the use of a set time interval between following trains, and when a 'special' was run a red flag had to be attached to its rear. Messages were given to trains by 'policemen,' usually former soldiers of good character, equipped with flags, who had at least on the MC a simple but comprehensive system of signals. Later, mechanical signals were used at the lineside to improve visibility. Shown in the delightful illustrations in the 'history' by Frederick Williams, these had a flat board atop a pole which could be turned to face the train as a stop signal. A variation used on the NM was designed to make it clear which line was being signalled. The electric telegraph was in its infancy and although trials had been undertaken on the Great Western it was not really reliable at that time. The pioneers forming the Midland did not use it so messages could not be passed between policemen. These 'Bobbies'—a term used to the present day for railway signalmen—must have been first-class men. Despite the complete lack of safety systems, accidents were few.

Early Train Services

Thirty-six InterCity 125s now thunder daily down the old MC line from Nottingham or Derby to London, twenty-one from the NM route starting from Sheffield, so that Nottingham is under two hours from London and Sheffield less than three.

Services in the 1840s were very different. The NM had only five weekday departures from Leeds to Derby, at 6.45am, 8.00am, 9.30am, 12.45pm, and 4.45pm, whose arrivals in the latter town were respectively 10.15am, 11.30am, 12.45pm, 4.15pm, and 8.15pm. Except the 9.30am 'express', they stopped at all twelve stations, while only the early and late departures carried third class passengers.

The elementary signalling of those days needed long time intervals between trains, but goods traffic would have made the gaps between succeeding services almost dangerously short.

At this time the NM was part of the trunk line south from Leeds through to London, with trains connecting at Derby with the MC to Rugby and then on via the L&B to London. The 'express' left York at 8.45am, making connections which would get a passenger to London at 7.30 in the evening. Three changes, with scant chance for refreshments were a small price to pay for halving the coach journey time of 20 hours, but the newspapers of the day complained bitterly that connections were usually missed at Rugby despite the timetable's assurance that passengers off the 'express' would be taken on from Rugby by 'Special Engines!'

The MC was more generous with its 'expresses' Half its six trains a day between Derby and Rugby missed the small intermediate stations such as Wigston (now a suburb of Leicester) but despite this Leicester to Derby took 75 minutes for 29 miles, an average of 23mph. The HSTs take just 25 minutes in far greater comfort. MC timetables also noted that 'carriage trucks and horse boxes will be kept at the principal stations, but to prevent disappointment, it is recommended that notice be given the previous day to the Clerk at the Station where they are required.'

Trouble and Strife

In the first years of the 1840s the infant lines faced with varying degrees of success all the operating and organisational problems of new railways. Most were solved without signposts to their solution, for none had travelled these paths before.

The problems were engineering, financial and operation; they were new because railways were new and because railway companies were something new in company size. No sooner had the lines been opened, operational problems solved, manning arranged, and agents appointed, than trouble started. The NM found that its expensive route over the South Yorkshire Hills had left it with crippling capital charges. The MC and the B&DJ ran into a different set of problems—competition! All three 'Derby' lines soon met all the ills of early railways—industrial strife, false promises by the managers, rate cutting, clashes of personality—all conspired to keep the shareholders awake at night. Worse was the in-fighting between the MC and the B&DJ.

For a few months before the MC opened, the B&DJ had all the

London traffic to itself, London trains connecting with the L&B at Hampton-in-Arden and taking just over seven hours to Euston. As soon as the MC opened this journey took an hour less via Leicester. The B&DJ lowered fares to catch trade, much to the distaste of the MC directors, who were a hard-headed lot. Over the next four years a fierce fares war flared up between these two companies; writs flew between Derby and Birmingham. Then the desperate MC directors' dirty tricks departments reached a secret agreement with the NM to book all through traffic via the MC to the exclusion of the B&DJ. Learning of this, the Birmingham company opposed an MC Bill in Parliament, withdrawing opposition only when the other two companies agreed to abandon their pact. Sullen agreement by the NM followed, to the further detriment of the Junction line.

While the three 'Derby' lines were squabbling, the L&B remained aloof, keeping an impartial attitude to passengers and connections from both the Junction and the Counties lines. This admirable attitude is revealed by a letter to the secretary of the B&DJ from the L&B saying:

'although this Company is interested in promoting the traffic which will pass over the longest portion of its line, they feel it is their duty in booking passengers through, whether by the Birmingham and Derby or by other lines, to act towards all with the most strict impartiality.'

Dividends were low. Just around two per cent was below that expected for returns on railway investment. From 1840 to 1844 the B&DJ averaged 1.6 per cent; the MC figure was marginally higher at 2.75 per cent, but both were much lower than the ten per cent averaged on the L&B.

The North Midland also suffered, not through competition, but due to the cost of driving a 'Stephenson line' with its easy gradients through the hilly country between Derby and Leeds, expensive at over £40,000 a mile; the MC cost only £15,000 a mile. Matters were not helped by the generous provision of stations, especially when we remember that the Leicester & Swannington passengers were booking fares at local inns. The result was a low dividend of 3.5 per cent – and a set of unhappy directors. Liverpool shareholders demanded a committee of inquiry. A little-known shareholder, George Hudson, joined and dominated the Committee, making radical proposals—closing three stations, Beighton, Killamarsh and Kilnhurst, sacking several officers, reducing wages, especially those of running staff, raising fares and selling surplus carriages. Drivers' wages were to be maintained at seven shillings (£0.35) a week but savings were made by longer working hours and a reduction in staffing levels. On objecting, all the drivers were laid off and fresh men engaged. Some of the new men had little experience; others had been dismissed from previous employment for lack of attention or for drinking on duty. Chaos followed; the new year's services of 1843 were in disarray, but the line just continued to function. A fatal accident at Barnsley, when an elderly driver failed to see a danger light, led the Government in the shape of the Trade Committee of the Privy Council to write to the company. The slimline NM won through, but at an unknown cost in terms of delayed trains and angry passengers. These sweeping re-forms were not adopted without a fight by Derby-based directors, who felt they were too drastic and inhuman. After a heated meeting at Leeds the proposals of the committee were carried, thanks to the eloquence and forcefulness of the newcomer, Hudson, elected with others on the investigating committee to the board, displacing the 'Derby Party.' The next moves in the NM game were so bound up in the personality and character of Hudson that we must go back to his early years.

George Hudson

A flawed genius who bestrode the railway stage during the 'Mania' of the 1840s, Hudson came to dominate by 1846 lines stretching from Newcastle to Bristol and from London to Cambridge and Colchester. The younger son of a prosperous farmer of Howsham, north of York, he was sent at 15 years of age to York to work in a draper's shop. George worked well, married into his employer's family, and became a partner in the profitable draper's shop, until his life was changed by a substantial legacy from a great uncle.

His money led him into the politics of York as a High Tory alderman, bringing him into contact with a committee formed to build a railway from York to London, and with George Stephenson. The two men became close friends until Stephenson's death. Hudson always took great heed of Stephenson's advice in railway engineering matters, and it must be admitted shamelessly used the great engineer's name in his schemes.

At that time a line all the way to London was not practical, but Hudson saw that a short line to join the planned North Midland would be feasible. Soon the provisional Committee of the York & North

Midland was formed with Hudson as treasurer and later chairman of the company, giving this remarkable man his foothold in the world of railways.

After some initial difficulties the line, planned under Stephenson's guidance, was started. Hudson, whose reputation in his native city rose to new heights, was elected Lord Mayor. His triumph was complete in 1839 when the Y&NM was opened as far as South Milford on the Leeds to Selby Railway.

Short of stature, well rounded by municipal hospitality, Hudson was a human dynamo. Leaving his drapery business in the care of family management, he threw himself into railway affairs. He was no office-bound company chairman, learning from his friend Stephenson the practical details of railway operation. He soon surpassed his teacher in his clear grasp of railway finances, especially when it came to saving pennies on wages and to the removal of unfortunate employees who asked for a living wage for reasonable hours of work. Hudson possessed the gift of mob oratory. This was important in the infant days of railway company management, for each joint stock company was a miniature democracy, with shareholders' votes counting for much.

Shareholders were small businessmen, farmers and professionals who knew little about railways but who wanted a good return on their capital. The large dominant landowners of the day took little interest in these new intrusions on their countryside, so their dominant voices were absent from company meetings, leaving the strident but well-informed voice of Hudson in the forefront. The York & North Midland was a line run by Hudson alone, with the assistance of his 'yes men' appointed to the board and planted carefully at shareholders' meetings amid the rank and file.

Hudson also possessed one other gift useful in dominating and manipulating small democracies—a scant regard for the truth, especially in financial affairs. In the 1840s it was not essential to have the books of a joint stock company audited; the watchword was 'every shareholder an auditor.' This world of early railways is a far cry from the large modern well-managed company, whose accounts are carefully audited and whose major shareholders are financially prudent pension funds, professionally controlled. Fortunately, in this new world of the joint stock railway company there was a major stabilising influence—the Quakers. Financially adventurous, yet prudent and above all honest, the Quakers invested heavily in railways and in other emerging industries. Edward Pease, the father of the Stockton & Darlington Railway was a Quaker, as was John Ellis, the joint founder of the Leicester & Swannington and a director of the Midland Counties. Through their corresponding network they provided a very beneficial influence on the railway world—honest, stable and hardworking.

Hudson at the North Midland

At a special meeting of NM shareholders in Leeds Hudson took control of the line. He installed his nominee as secretary, and appointed a former Yorkshire & North Midland man as locomotive and operating superintendent. Wages were reduced, and less experienced but cheaper employees hired. The result was a fatal accident and a public outcry. Nevertheless, Hudson had promised savings, so ruthless economies were applied. *The Railway Times* wrote:

'Office after office has been abolished, check after check has been abandoned, accounts have been voted useless and a rapid concentration of all offices including the directional functions is taking place in the person of one individual.'

Despite the economies, finances were slow to improve and shareholders became restive, so Hudson used the classic trick of the 'moving target.' He would change the rules of the game before his lack of success could surface. Hudson then moved with consumate cunning. Acting on a sensible suggestion made by Robert Stephenson that the best way to solve the financial problems of the three Derby-based lines was to amalgamate them, Hudson secretly started negotiations with the B&DJ board. He proposed complete amalgamation of all three companies, on the basis of equal shares in the new amalgamated line, but with reduced dividend provision for the smaller B&DJ. Hudson knew that the hard-headed MC directors would oppose this move, and he with great cunning, in secret meetings between the NM and the B&DJ set up a takeover of the Junction line by the NM which would have the effect of syphoning all Leeds to London traffic away from the MC, ruining that company. News leaked out, and B&DJ shares rose rapidly without apparent cause.

On 1 August 1843, Hudson presented the directors of the MC with an ultimatum—either they accepted the amalgamation or the MC would lose most of its traffic! The MC board held fast behind its proud and stubborn Chairman, Dicey, and a special shareholders' meeting was held to discuss the moves. Hudson played the meeting beautifully, appealing to the shareholders over the heads of the board. With a superb combination of rhetoric and an unrivalled grasp of the details of railway finances, Hudson convinced the MC shareholders, and the amalgamation went ahead—just in time to avoid awkward questions about the savings in operating the NM!

The new railway, formed in the first-ever railway amalgamation was called THE MIDLAND RAILWAY.

3

THE YOUNG MIDLAND

The New Railway

On 10 May 1844 the new railway 'The Midland' was incorporated by Act of Parliament. At 170 miles it was the longest railway in England and the first to be formed by amalgamation. The first meeting of directors held appropriately in the Derby station offices elected Hudson as chairman, and by an act of great good fortune for the new line, John Ellis as deputy chairman. These men formed a strong team—the daring and imaginative Hudson ready to take short cuts to achieve his ends, and the Quaker, Ellis, a shrewd businessman insisting on the highest standards of ethics at a time when company law was in its infancy and dishonesty was rife in railways circles.

As in most amalgamations, inevitably there were 'removals from office'. The secretary of the B&DJ, James Allport, could not be found a suitable post. Hudson spotted his talents and obtained a post for him on one of his Northern lines. We shall hear more of him later! The Locomotive Superintendent of the same line, Matthew Kirtley, was luckier and was retained a little surprisingly as the Locomotive & Carriage Superintendent of the new company. He did stirling work for his new masters.

The new railway with Hudson at the helm was in a commanding position, holding the key to railway travel between London and the North of England. All traffic to Leeds and Newcastle, and hence to Scotland, used the Midland Railway between Rugby and Normanton, then a bustling junction. The rival West Coast route to Scotland through Lancashire and Cumberland, although preferred by a Parliamentary Committee, was unfinished, slowed down by the mountains of the Lake District. This calm and confident position was to be broken soon by two great battles—one to be won and one to be lost—the Battle of the Gauges and the war to stop a London to York direct line. At the formation of the Midland the possibility of a York direct line taking away northern traffic was well in the future, but the battle of the gauges had started!

The War of the Gauges

If we take a look at the railway map of England in 1840–1, we see a network growing at a rate which would put the 20th Century road builders to shame. The map shows a clutch of lines in the north-east (where railways started), routes south from Leeds and Lancaster to London meeting at Rugby, a line to Southampton in the south, and a single line snaking west toward Bristol. All these except the Bristol line were planned by the Stephensons, father and son, and members of their 'school' of railway engineering—flat lines of a maximum gradient of 1 in 300 to allow for the small locomotive engines of the time, and a strange gauge of 4 ft 8½in, derived from the practice of the Newcastle coalfield. There were a few exceptions to the easy gradients when the lie of the land needed a length of steeper path, but the gauge was always the same.

The London to Bristol line was surveyed by a towering genius, Isambard Kingdom Brunel, who was not prepared to accept a gauge so narrow, and who maintained that trains would run smoother and faster using a gauge of 7ft. After some debate the line to Bristol was built to that 'broad' gauge. Brunel's line spawned others, to Exeter and beyond, into South Wales and to Cheltenham and Gloucester. It was inevitable that these gauges would meet and meet they did, at Gloucester. England is too small a country to have two gauges, so Parliament decided to rule on the appropriate width and set off a struggle which lasted ten years.

Macdermot, the historian of the Great Western Railway, summed up this whole conflict thus:

'What has usually been called "The Battle of the Gauges" was really a long war, lasting some ten years from the first meeting of the two gauges at Gloucester in 1844. During this war many battles were fought with varying results before the Broad Gauge forces were at last defeated by the mere multitude of their enemies.'

The Midland was drawn in almost by accident and we must first go back a few years to 1832 when the Sturges, Quaker brothers of Birmingham, saw that a railway from their native town to Bristol, then a port of almost equal rank to London and Liverpool, would help the rapidly growing factories of the West Midlands.

They employed the very young Brunel to survey a line, but as was often the case investment was slow to come and Brunel's line was never built. A few years later a Captain Moorsom, the brother of a later chairman of the London & North Western Railway, surveyed a new route. Moorsom took the line down from Birmingham as far as Gloucester, a useful port on the Severn. He avoided the major towns of Worcester, Droitwich and Tewkesbury, whose city fathers were all opposed to the railway. Cheltenham welcomed the line and prospered from it.

The Birmingham & Gloucester Railway's was the first railway Bill ever to be passed at the initial attempt, due to the careful choice of route. This line was at odds with the Stephenson 'flat line' concept and included a length at the severe gradient of 1 in 37. Generations of locomotive firemen were to curse this stretch, as they struggled to maintain steam up the Lickey Bank.

The line from Birmingham down to Cheltenham was easily built from a temporary terminus at Camp Hill, Birmingham, in 1840. As a junction with the other Birmingham lines was planned, the gauge was the standard 4ft 8½in.

The story becomes much more complex when we start talking about the stretch of the Birmingham & Gloucester Railway between Cheltenham and Gloucester. This confusion was due to the inability of the lawyers of the time to understand the concept of a joint line of railway. Now a company called the Cheltenham & Great Western Union had been formed to build a line from the small village of Swindon to Cheltenham and to Gloucester. Formed in close collaboration with the GWR, its Act was passed only two months after that of the B&G. The stretch between the two Gloucestershire towns, only six miles long and based on an old tramway, was to be common to the B&G and the C&GWU. Later, many joint lines were built, but this was the first and it caused the lawyers some problems! The Parliamentary draughtsmen came up with a tortuous arrangement by which the line was owned by the C&GWU, which acted as trustees for the B&G for the half of the line nearest Gloucester. The Birmingham company, according to Macdermot, was to make the depot at Gloucester at its own cost for the use of both, the Cheltenham company leasing it the land required, while the latter company was to make a common depot at Cheltenham. What a mess!

The Act for the line between Cheltenham and Gloucester called for the rails to be of the same standard gauge as the B&G. The C&GWU was a broad gauge line, so the first ever mixed-gauge section was laid between the two towns. Time constraints were placed on the

41

C&GWU line to ensure that all the line to Gloucester would be opened at the same time as that between Birmingham and Cheltenham. The Union company defaulted on this and the mixed gauge portion was bought by the Birmingham company at £20,000 a month before the opening from Gloucester through to Camp Hill, Birmingham, in 1840.

The Bristol and Gloucester

This already complex plot now thickens even more! In 1839, an Act had been obtained by a company truly independent of the GWR to transform a standard gauge tramway built to take coals from Coal Pit Heath to Bristol, into a line from Bristol to Gloucester, so completing the line from Birmingham to Bristol. The line was to join the C&GWU at Standish, a few miles south of Cheltenham and Gloucester. The original gauge of the line was to have been standard, but just before laying the rails the Great Western took over the GWU line, giving the directors of the B&G cause for thought. They would have the broad gauge at both ends of their line. Use of the broad gauge would allow them to use the new GWR station at Temple Meads, Bristol, one of the finest in England. Brunel, as engineer to the line, probably helped the directors change to the broad gauge. The new line was also to have the use of the C&GW (now GWR) terminus at Gloucester.

Gloucester found itself in a complex of lines built in the 19th Century manner, without a clear plan. The layout was awkward and has left a difficult legacy to this day, with this important town placed at the end of a 'branch' off the Bristol to Birmingham line. This awkward layout has persisted down the years, in effect leaving Gloucester without an inter-city service to London.

In the 1840s things were even worse—the two gauges met at Gloucester, served by two adjoining stations, one for the B&G, the other for the C&GWU. Any through traffic, goods or passenger had to transfer between the two Gloucester stations, truly a recipe for disaster!

Chaos at Gloucester

As soon as goods traffic started to run between Birmingham and Bristol on 2 September 1844 the problems caused by the transfer at Gloucester became very real. Transfer was needed for each waggon between the two adjacent stations, and soon chaos reigned. The narrow gauge lines, the L&B, the Grand Junction, and the Midland, started a public relations campaign to make the inconvenience of the broad gauge widely known. Soon a Parliamentary Commission was formed to investigate the gauge question. In one famous incident, the Commissioners visited Gloucester to see for themselves. Hearing of this the goods manager of the B&G hurried to Gloucester to prepare a feast of disorder for their viewing, a contemporary writer describing the chaos graphically:

'Fearing lest the extent of the transfer work might be too small to impress the Committee, he arranged for the unloading of two trains already dealt with, as an addition to the usual work and when the members came to see the scene they were appalled by the clamour arising from the well arranged confusion'.

The railway journals of the time and the press made much of the Gloucester difficulties. It might be thought that the profession of 'public relations' is an invention of the 20th Century—yet the narrow gauge protagonists employed at least one pamphlet writer to stir up opinion against the broad gauge interests.

By January 1845 the two lines at Gloucester had amalgamated, forming the Bristol & Birmingham Railway. The Great Western was keen to extend its sphere of influence by incorporating the new railway into its camp, especially as the B&B ran into the Curzon Street terminus of the L&B—the high priests of the narrow gauge faction! The B&B would have been a valuable prize for the broad gauge and even the cry 'broad gauge to the Mersey' was heard. The GWR offered £60 for each £100 B&B share—in reality £67, as GWR shares were at a good premium. The B&B held out for £65 and the meeting between the two parties was adjourned for three days. Meanwhile in a drama worthy of any television series John Ellis, the deputy chairman of the Midland, by chance met Edmund Sturges and Joseph Gibbons, directors of the B&B, on the London train. Ellis taking his professional life in his hands, pledged the Midland to better terms than the GWR and secured the line to the Midland and to the narrow gauge interests! In his own words, 'I had better run the risk of losing a few thousand pounds than admit the plague of the broad gauge to Birmingham'. Ellis was swift-footed, but completely ethical in his fast and shrewd move.

The 'gauge war' was not lost on that day—it rumbled on for ten years until the Oxford, Worcester & Wolverhampton Railway (the

'Old Worse and Worse') mutinied in the early 1850s and used the standard gauge. After that England lost one of Brunel's greatest contributions to travel, the comfortable, safe and fast broad gauge trains.

The Bristol line transformed the Midland from a purely local concern into a national railway—Ellis' chance conversation was very far reaching!

In 1848 the Midland attempted to introduce the mixed gauge to Bristol by adding a third rail to the section of their line between Standish Junction and Temple Meads. They were stopped in the House of Lords by GW interests. In the event, ten years of confusion reigned at Gloucester before there was no break of gauge between Birmingham and Bristol.

It is something of a mystery why the Midland, well entrenched as it was in the narrow gauge camp, tolerated the break of gauge within its system. Certainly the GWR interests kept the narrow gauge out of Bristol as long as possible. The true reason probably lies in the fact that railway directors of the Hudson era (Ellis excepted) cared little for passengers' interests. A fight to drive 4ft 8½in lines to Bristol was something that the Midland Board avoided in the first troubled years of its new railway.

Today Gloucester still pays the penalty for the haphazard ways of the early builders. Because its station lies on the route to Newport and South Wales rather than the route to London, it is served in effect by a branch from Swindon. The trains to Cheltenham and the Marches by-pass this active town, well provided by major roads. The Midland had built an expensive line across the roofs of the pleasant cathedral city to avoid Birmingham–Bristol trains having to reverse. This line is now disused, leaving Gloucester ill-served.

Services and Locomotives on the Bristol Line

Much of the traffic along the B&B was between Bristol and the Midlands; all passengers and goods had to change at Gloucester for ten years until the GWR and the Midland agreed that the mixed gauge could be laid. Services were typical of the times; only six trains ran each day carrying passengers. The fastest took over three hours on the Bristol to Birmingham run, including the change of trains at Gloucester. Today's InterCity 125s do the 93 miles in just over the hour.

The line encompassed a great novel feature, the Lickey Bank, 1 in 37 of line which taxed locomotives until the coming of diesels in the late 1950s.

The B&B engineer Moorsom imported special 4-2-0s built by Norris of Philadelphia to work the Lickey, buying 14 of these locomotives on the flimsy grounds that North American railways had experience of such inclines. The Norris locomotives were built on what was to become the standard North American pattern—a front bogie to follow the curving and irregular track, with driving wheels placed far back to get high adhesion, and frames on the Bury pattern. As both Stephenson and Bury had declined to supply locomotives for the Lickey duties, Moorsom did well with these imports. They worked the bank well, although some of the lighter design at 9 tons were found wanting and did not last long. The 12ton locomotives served well into Midland days. J. E. McConnell, locomotive superintendent of the B&B, who later did distinguished work on the Southern section of the LNWR, converted most of them into saddle tanks.

One less successful locomotive bought from the Grand Junction, called 'Dr Church's engine,' blew up near the Lickey in one of the earliest recorded boiler explosions. The cause of the explosion is unknown, but possibly the driver was tempted to raise his boiler pressure by screwing down the locomotive's safety valve. Later, the Ramsbottom safety valve would have prevented this 'aid' to power up the Lickey. The driver and fireman are buried in Bromsgrove churchyard, but unfortunately their tombstone had depicted a Norris locomotive instead of this unique engine.

Beware—The Great Northern Cometh

The newly amalgamated Midland had little time at peace before a most serious rival to its fortunes was mooted. The merchants of Leeds had become concerned that their town was becoming a railway backwater. York, thanks to Hudson, was the new northern centre of the railway network, leaving Leeds stranded on a branch off the grand York and Derby line from the Northumberland coalfields to the South and the rich London markets. Moreover Doncaster, a town of some importance, had been spurned by the Hudson party and was languishing away from rail connections. Edmund Dennison, born in Leeds and practising law in Doncaster, rose to the occasion and led a company to plan a Direct York Line, with a major route to Leeds from Doncaster. Dennison was a man in the heroic mould of the day; determined and ambitious, he and Hudson were bitter personal rivals who on one occasion had a public row on York station.

After two false starts and two engineers later, a line was at last surveyed and proposals laid before Parliament. Sweeping majestically up the flat Eastern Counties of England, it avoided the industrial Midlands, passing through Peterborough (making its fortune, in contrast to the nearby ancient coaching centre of Stamford, which became a pleasant backwater), Grantham, Retford and Doncaster. The line was intended to carry on to York but linked up instead with a cross-country route to York at Askern junction.

Now Hudson, in collaboration with Robert Stephenson, had carefully amalgamated a series of small Northumberland railways to form the York, Newcastle & Berwick, forging a route to London for the rich Newcastle coal traffic via the Hudson-controlled Y&NM and the Midland. The last thing wanted by the Midland was a direct York to London link!

The battle was on as soon as the GN Bill was placed before the newly constituted Board of Trade Committee for The Classification of Railway Bills. Hudson mounted a two-forked attack on his interests: first by opposing the GN Bill in Parliament with all the considerable power at his disposal, and second by projecting two new lines, cutting right across the new GN route—the Nottingham to Lincoln and the Leicester to Peterborough.

In Parliament battle was joined before the Board of Trade Committee, then chaired by a brilliant young politician, Lord Dalhousie. This remarkable man who cut his railway teeth on the GN Bill was soon to become Viceroy of India, using his experience to plan a superb system of lines for the sub-continent, built with Government support to the sensible gauge of 5ft 6in. His memory lives today in the superb Delhi railway museum, honoured as the father of Indian Railways.

George Stephenson opposed the GN Bill before the Committee on the grounds of severe gradients and the high cost of land for its King's Cross, London, terminus. The Committee agreed with Stephenson, then at the height of his influence, but Parliament was afraid of the dangers of monopoly and was set on maximising railway competition. Thirty-two expensive counsel were deployed on both sides, helped by witnesses beyond count, backed up by an army of clerks. Easily the biggest battle fought in Parliament over a railway Bill, Hudson could not use his great gifts of oratory directly as only counsel could address the Committee. At one stage he was banished from the meeting, one noble Lord observing 'the only sovereign entitled to be present was Her Majesty. The railway potentate had no right to be there.'

Spending £3,000 a day on fees alone, Hudson held up the GN Bill for 75 days. Meanwhile the two Midland Bills were passed, without blocking the GN Bill, which also passed the Committee by the Chairman's casting vote.

Hudson then used his last card. A minion with the appropriate name of Croucher examined the subscription lists of the GN in minute detail to discover that no less than £29,000 worth of shares were held by people with no means of paying their calls. However, Parliament prevailed and the Midland's great rival was born.

The 'Railway King' now turned his attentions to the new railway and by great cunning became an ally, turning his Y&NM into a feeder to the GN. In 1847 he craftily promoted a short line from the Y&NM at Burton Salmon to a precursor of the Lancashire & Yorkshire at Knottingly, supposedly to serve limestone quarries. This offered the now impoverished GN, bled white by Parliamentary costs, a ready route over the Y&NM to York. The Midland directors were not at all amused by Hudson's desertion of their cause as soon as the GN battle was lost; they turned on him and destroyed him.

The Mania

The Midland was born at a time in the development of the railways of England that may be termed interesting if not downright turbulent. Fortune smiled, trade was reviving, and money was looking for profitable homes. Thanks to a reduction to five per cent on the money needed 'up front' for new railway promotion, much of that cash was going into railways. A combination of factors which were only imperfectly understood led to a massive increase in the new lines put up for Parliamentary approval in 1844–45. A great wave of railway speculation—much dishonest—swept through the land. The second and greatest 'Mania' had started. In 1845 and in the two following sessions no fewer than 900 Bills were examined by a special Parliamentary Committee on The Classification of Railway Bills. Over 400 were looked at in 1846 alone, leading 'The Thunderer' (as *The Times* was commonly known) to publish a supplement violently opposing the new fashion for railway speculation. In dramatic prose the editor, W. F. Spackman, listed all the railways built and projected in Great Britain, amounting to £701 million, a sum which accounted for most of the national wealth of England at the time! Spackman's cautionary tale, part of a much-needed campaign to tighten up the incredibly slack company law of the time, was well conceived and was heeded by the authorities. Not all was speculation for a quick profit. Railway mileage, much of it well-built and profitable, increased from 2,000 in 1844 to 6,000 by 1850. The two decades from 1830 to 1850 saw the novelty of the Leicester & Swannington change to the established basis of the enormous industrial growth of Great Britain in the mid 19th Century. The growth was mercifully not held back by central planning as in France, and was able to go full speed ahead until the money ran out by 1850.

Inevitably, some men flourished on the 'Mania'—others lost all. One lawyer made the immense sum of £40,000 in one year, had a nervous breakdown, and retired to the country on the proceeds of his railway legal fees. The 'Mania' gave Hudson—a typical, brash, self-made railway promoter with a scant regard for proper accounting proceedures—the chance to exploit every trick to extract money from unsuspecting investors. His favourite trick was to pay dividends from new capital, giving lines a false façade of prosperity. On basically profitable lines this could be sustained, but with the rural and poverty-stricken railways of East Anglia the results were disastrous, lingering on even today, as any traveller from Norfolk will avow. Fortunately for the Midland, the financial probity of the deputy chairman kept Hudson's sharp practice out of bounds.

Hudson put up a magnificent front. Member of Parliament for Sunderland, he held court at a large mansion at Albert Gate, London, which is now the French Embassy. At the height of his powers he controlled in a tight grip and to his personal advantage lines from Newcastle to Bristol, and covering much of East Anglia. Even the Duke of Wellington—who lived nearby at 'No 1 London'—called on Hudson for help, in the latter's heyday. The Duke's sister had foolishly speculated in a poor line whose shares fell, almost ruining her. Hudson bought the shares in a public manner, pushing up their value, and saving her fortune. The Duke in return called on Hudson's daughter at her school, raising her social standing markedly. Hudson's influence was not wholly bad. He worked to a strategy to forge a grand link from London to Edinburgh. North of the Border the railways were firmly Scottish, but in the North East Hudson's alliance with Robert Stephenson welded an assortment of loss-making small Northumberland lines into a trunk route feeding traffic down the York, Newcastle & Berwick to the Y&NM and the Midland to London. A good Member of Parliament, he set up industries in Sunderland to supply the railways with the materials they needed, glass for carriages, and general engineering. He founded the ship-yards which made the town prosperous until the 1930s.

In the end, though, the reckoning came. Hudson had 'robbed Peter to pay Paul' for too long and his debts were called in by a growing band of suspicious shareholders. Lambert in his admirable *Life of Hudson, The Railway King*, lists his considerable debts at the time of his dethronement. Hudson denied all, but he was forced to resign from all his boards, including that of the Midland. His 'yes men' were removed as well, no longer protecting him from the new directorates. The Y&NM and the YN&B persisted in the pursuit of their money. Hudson remained a free man while still in Parliament, but a political change and his diminished reputation unseated him. Fleeing from his creditors to Paris, he lived in genteel poverty for some years until the citizens of Whitby arranged an annuity to enable him to live in some slight comfort in his old age.

The Lincoln Branch

While Parliament was still debating the GN Bill the Midland branch to Lincoln was approved. Designed as a 'stopper' this line is now a most valuable link to the busy city of Lincoln and pays its way as an important coal feeder line to the massive power stations in the Trent Valley. Not a meandering route through rural backwaters like many railways built purely to impede a rival's plans it is in part an InterCity line, joining its former deadly rival the GN at Retford. Easy to build, it ran over the flat plain of the Trent to the market town of Retford and beyond to Lincoln. At the Nottingham end, the former Midland Counties terminus had to be changed from a terminus to accommodate Lincoln trains by adding a platform at the south side of the station. Trains left Nottingham to cause great congestion at a road level crossing just to the east of the former terminus, before running through tranquil country to Newark. This stretch of level, straight, not over-used line was the site of the famous brake trials, of which more later. Stations were in the Tudor cottage style much adorned with bargeboards. For some reason Fiskerton and Rolleston Junction were placed within a mile of each other, generous provision for a rural cross-country railway. An interesting branch left the direct route at this junction, bound for the small cathedral city of Southwell. Full of character, redolent of a minor ecclesiastical seat, the 'Suth'll Paddy' connected well with the Nottingham and Lincoln services, enabling Nottingham notables to commute to their distinguished posts from that pleasant city. In the early days trains on the branch were horse-drawn, but a through line to Mansfield built in the 1870s by the Midland for coal traffic boosted the branch. The station was rebuilt and trains ran to places as far away as Buxton at the behest it is rumoured of the Bishop, the better to visit his widely spread flock. The 'Suth'll' lent itself to stories of flower picking from the slow-moving shuttle and of visits to local inns while steam was raised. Such lines, unfortunately, exist no more.

Beyond Newark the line ran nearly straight to terminate at Lincoln St Marks in the water meadows in the shadow of Lincoln's great and beautiful cathedral. The railway saved Lincoln from obscurity; once the most influential city in middle England, its diocese stretching as far as Oxford, it could have decayed into a rural backwater. Instead the railway made it into a thriving market centre and a manufacturing base for the prosperous Lincolnshire wolds.

The Battle of Saxby

The other blocking line devised by Hudson to thwart the Great Northern Bill is also very much alive today. Hudson did not believe in useless lines! Leaving the old Midland Counties line at Syston, it follows the River Wreake to Melton Mowbray, winding its way down to Oakham in what was the County of Rutland, up through Stamford and on to Peterborough. Built through much more hilly country than the Lincoln branch, the Peterborough line wandered to catch what population there was, and to keep earthworks to a minimum. The local all-powerful landlords had a particularly strong influence on this line, causing havoc and mayhem. Landlords were always a force to be reckoned with, but they could usually be bought off—not so with the Peterborough branch!

Stamford had been an importance place since the Danes ruled this part of England, and the town was an important coaching stop on the Great North Road to Scotland. The town, controlled by the Cecil family, was hemmed in to the south by their home, Burley Park, and to the north by the Cecil farmlands. Popular legend has it that when the GN was under survey the Cecil family feared that the railway would cause overcrowding and insurrection in the town, the like of which had not been seen in Nottingham since the turn of the century. The family's influence in Parliament was so great it is said that it was able to persuade the GN promoters to lay out their line to pass through the cathedral city of Peterborough, a few miles to the south-east of Stamford.

The results of their actions were far-reaching; Stamford became a pleasant rural backwater, Peterborough grew. Today they are greatly different places, one a pleasant small town, the home of professionals working in Peterborough and even as far away as London and Leicester. Peterborough grew to be a not unpleasant, manufacturing centre with a major InterCity station on the old GN main line. Hudson, though, was able to persuade the Cecil family to accept the Leicester to Peterborough branch. Perhaps his High Tory politics helped, and the Midland brought the railway to Stamford.

At the other end of the branch Hudson's surveyors faced real opposition in the person of the powerful and strong-minded Lord Harborough. He flatly rejected all Hudson's overtures, posting notices around his seat, Stapleford Park, forbidding entry of all railway agents and surveyors. His dislike of railways was not entirely due to prejudice; he owned much of the threatened Oakham Canal. The Midland men, not to be thwarted by such tactics, recruited Nottingham prize fighters to protect them. The ensuing 'Battle of Saxby' between the Harborough gamekeepers and the Midland men lasted three days, ending with protagonists from both sides in Leicester Jail!

The Midland lost the battle but won the war, going to the courts to gain their route. Even after the passing of the Syston to Peterborough Act in June 1845, Lord Harborough was so opposed to the railway that the Midland laid out a sharply curved deviation away from Stapleford Park. Even this displeased the lord. When a 150-strong survey party entered his property he led a charge of gamekeepers and farmworkers, routing the railwaymen. Eventually, law and order were restored and the line was built with the notorious 'Lord Harborough's curve' slowing trains to walking pace. Later, when this line became part of a trunk route to Nottingham, the curve was eased, and its remains can be seen today alongside those of the now-defunct canal.

The Nudge to the North

The Midland directors saw clearly from its earliest days that the railway needed to break out of its central hemmed-in position in England's industrial heartland. Long-distance traffic and travel was growing. National instead of local railways were emerging, which would leave the Midland a hostage to its surrounding competitors. In the late 1840s and early 1850s finances would not stretch to major expansions, so a highly desirable thrust to the north was replaced by a nudge.

In 1844 an independent line was approved to connect Leeds to

Bradford—surveyed by Stephenson, it was a typical valley line using the Aire. Only one tunnel was needed at the cost of a rather round-about route, entering Bradford from the north. By 1850 it was losing money, a matter of great concern to its Yorkshire owners. Committees of inquiry were formed; investigations ensued, economies were suggested, sackings proposed, and above all a lease to a more powerful and professionally managed line mooted. The first in the field was the Leeds & Manchester, later to become the Lancashire & Yorkshire. Terms were complex and difficult to agree, so Hudson stepped in with scant reference to his Midland board, proposing a generous ten per cent guaranteed dividend, snapped up by the grateful L&B directors. Hudson made a personal 'killing' out of this deal, and forged what was to be the first nail in his coffin in the process. The lease became effective just after his demise from active direction of the Midland, but as usual he had a nose for a winner. Never a financial winner, nevertheless the L&B gave the Midland a vital exit to the north, later to be part of the great Settle to Carlisle run, when the L&B built a short extension as far as Skipton. The deal destroyed any hope of a single central station in Bradford, for the L&B had built its terminus, Market Street, at the northern end of Bradford's hilly central district, whereas the L&YR station was south of centre. A plan to link them failed at the lease. The Midland later made amends and gave Bradford fine services in the comfortable trains of its later prosperous years.

The second benefit from this useful little line was in Leeds itself. The NM had a terminus well out of the centre at Hunslet, but the L&B had a terminus at Wellington in the centre of town, the first to be built there. Wellington always was much better than the station shared by the GN and the L&Y nearby, called 'Central.' Both are now combined in a modern station, light, airy and convenient for the traveller. The author well remembers the horror of the old stations in post-war years when connections were frequently lost at Leeds just looking for the right station!

The Wellington station, unlike its modern replacement and the rival GN/L&YR joint station was a terminus, built with seven platforms. Always a busy place, in the 1900s there were 120 daily trains out and 116 inward. Much used by commercial travellers in the days before car travel, the 'left luggage' was usually overflowing with samples of their wares.

For a short while after its opening even the dreaded GN trains used Wellington. The GN gained entry to Leeds via Manchester and Leeds (later the L&Y) under running powers given over Midland tracks for a few miles out of Leeds before handing them over to the NM at

Normanton. When the L&Y met the GN with a junction at Askern, the L&Y retained the running powers into Wellington station. The Midland denied the legality of this move, so the Manchester company resorted to a cunning strategy, advertising in 1849 that it would as usual run its St Leger specials to Doncaster from Leeds, and felt 'compelled to borrow' GN stock for this traffic! At the last minute the Midland local management discovered that the GN stock would also include GN locomotives driven by GN crews. In the robust manner of the day, the Midland responded by pulling up rails at the junction with the L&M near Methley. Nevertheless the Midland under duress at last agreed to let the arch rival GN and its new ally the L&Y into the Midlands Leeds station. Later the GN and the L&Y built their own Leeds through station near to the Midland terminus, proving to be a major shambles designed to confuse the unwary traveller.

The 'Little North Western'

As soon as the L&B settled down it built an extension up to Skipton, near the Brontë country north-west of Leeds, close by the watershed between the Aire flowing east down into Leeds and the Ribble flowing west to the Irish Sea. This gave the railway builders a chance to engineer an east-west route without crossing the Pennines proper. The promoters also envisaged a line cutting up to meet the Lancaster & Carlisle, a rather rebellious client railway beholden to the Grand Junction, soon to become the LNWR. The proposed line was called the North Western, known later as the 'Little North Western.'

As it happened, only the route between Skipton and Lancaster was built, with a later branch at the 'little' Clapham Junction to Low Gill on the LNWR West Coast main line. An important extension beyond Lancaster to Morecambe and to a new harbour at Heysham followed.

A ramshackle affair, the Little North Western did not prosper; traffic away from the industrial heartlands was sparse. When it opened, owing to failure to make any provision for rolling stock, the line was worked under contract by Edmund Sharpe, a former company secretary, at a rate of eleven pence (0.05) a mile for the four trains a day each way between Skipton and Lancaster. Sharpe later was given a contract to build a number of carriages for the line, an enterprise fraught with disaster as he built them to a loading gauge more attuned to the broad gauge than the North Western, whose board had a hard time with this contractor, on one occasion informing him that all his passenger stock was unsafe. Things did not improve, and he was told in 1852 that the board had come to a traffic arrangement with the Midland, which took over a motley collection of second-hand locomotives and worn out carriages, bought from Sharpe for around £1,000 each. Despite the arrangement between the NW and the Midland, the larger railway did little to protect the smaller line, the Midland passing scant traffic through Lancaster. Eventually, as will be seen later, the Midland was in a position to take over the line completely, building a joint line to Carnforth with the Furness Railway.

Today the Skipton to Settle portion forms part of the Settle to Carlisle run. The joint Midland Railway and Furness Railway branch remains, but the Lancaster line closed in 1962. On the positive side, the harbour at Heysham thrives with comfortable sailings twice a day to the Isle of Man. In fact this harbour, with its nuclear power station and Isle of Man car ferry is a picture of bustle and prosperity. The old joint FR line just survives, with a mere eight trains a day calling at the 'other' Clapham junction, not greatly different from the 1903 timetable, when just ten called. Since 1962 when the Lancaster branch closed, this Clapham has not been a junction.

The Midland in the late Forties

By 1849 the great railway building boom was on the wane and railways were employing more workers to run the services than building new track. The immense power of the engineers, men such as Brunel and the Stephensons, was giving way to a new generation of professional managers. The first, Charles Saunders, had been appointed on the GWR as early as 1840, Mark Huish on the LNWR from its inception in 1846. Often military men, their skills were needed to run the new enlarged railways, now growing into organisations much bigger in manpower, income and complexity then any other British firms.

By 1850 the management of the Midland was still very much in the hands of the Chairman of the Board, John Ellis. The dominating Hudson had not long departed and the era of highly competent professional managers had not yet reached the Midland. Three years were to pass before the highly professional James Allport would be appointed to the General Manager's post, nine years after leaving the B&DJ at the amalgamation with the other two Derby lines.

Ellis ruled justly and fairly over Britain's longest railway, 434 miles from Leeds to Bristol and Rugby. Its first rival in size was the LNWR serving the North West, 385 miles long and surpassing the Eastern Counties Railway's surprising 247 miles, pushing the GWR at 231 miles into fourth place.

We know quite a lot about the finances of the mid-century Midland Railway; the Government had started taking statistics! The Midland cost nearly £9½ million to build, while its plant, locomotives, carriages and waggons accounted for £1.7 million. The Midland had avoided paying London property prices; its earthworks were modest by the standards of the LNWR (with its Kilsby tunnel) and the Lancashire & Yorkshire's expensive route across the Pennines. The Midland's construction cost of £23,059 per mile was modest set beside the monumental £46,808 of the poverty-stricken South Eastern Railway, with its expensive terminus at London Bridge, and compared well with the £42,481 per mile of the Lancashire line. Still, to be realistic, the ordinary traveller was not in the least concerned about who ran the railway, or how. His main concern was firstly the cost of his journey. The 'Parliamentary' fare laid down in Gladstone's Bill at one penny a mile on at least one train a day was high at a time when the average semi-skilled worker only earned ten shillings (50p) a week. The single fare from Leeds to London would have cost him more than a week's wages. His modern equivalent takes but a day to earn his fare to London! Next he would notice with relief that the third class carriages had changed greatly for the better since Mr Gladstone's Act. Before, on the MC, thirds were little more than open waggons with crude seats. Now he would climb into a four-wheeler seating 30 passengers, which was closed to the wind and rain. The door windows could be opened or kept shut if needed, with a framed glass window falling into a recess in the door when ventilation was required. The carriage was lighted with an Argand oil lamp—luxury compared with the early days. When the train started it was slow—taking 3¼ hours for the 50 miles from Rugby to Derby, over 4½ hours for the 73 miles from Derby to Leeds. If he was unlucky, though, he might travel in one of the old seconds made into a third—they had no glazing in the side openings. In 1850, though, the anticipated increase in traffic due to the Great Exhibition caused the Midland to order many more thirds. The gentry travelling on the same train would have more room, 8 or 10 passengers in the same space, and upholstered seats. An early photograph shows a very early Midland first class coupé, only 4ft 9in wide, probably transferred to a new frame. The body, dating back to pre-amalgamation days has a close resemblance to a stage coach. Luggage was stowed on top; footwarmers were not provided until the

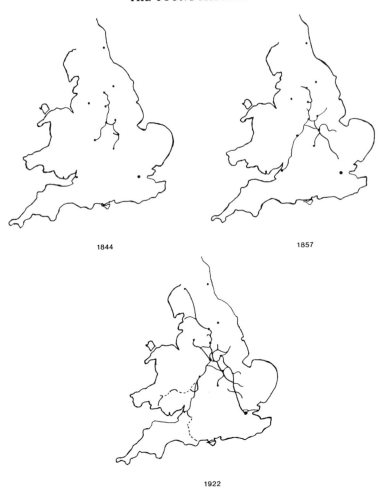

1844

1857

1922

Growth of the Midland Railway system

mid-1850s, so all had a cold journey in winter. The train might also have had a couple of horseboxes and a carriage trunk to take the gentrys' conveyances down to London. The third class traveller's boss in the second class was not all that comfortable, and he paid the extra to travel second out of social custom more than anything else.

Our traveller would certainly have spent some time looking at the varied locomotives, collected from four small concerns, each having made its own experiments with the changing and developing designs of the 1840s.

More of the travellers were 'thirds' than the railways had expected. They travelled short distances, a few miles on average. The average 'third' would be going to see relatives in the next town, finding work, or be on one of the growing number of special excursions to local events pioneered by Thomas Cook.

Early Midland Rolling Stock

The new Midland Railway inherited from its constituent companies 95 locomotives, 282 carriages, 1,256 goods wagons, plus an assortment of horseboxes, post office vans and carriage trucks.

The locomotives were a very mixed bag—tiny Bury 0-4-0s from the Midland Counties, sturdy sandwich-framed 2-2-2s from the North Midland and the Birmingham & Derby Junction, and a motley collection from the small Sheffield & Rotherham Railway. The acquisition of the Leicester & Swannington was to add some robust, but underpowered 0-6-0s and the Gloucester lines would add the American banking engines, and even a few broad gauge locomotives. The new locomotive superintendent was in a hurry to form a fleet from this motley collection, capable of powering the growing traffic of the young Midland. On amalgamation, Hudson had three only to choose from for this post: Josiah Kersley from the MC, Thomas Kirtley of the NM and his younger brother, Matthew, the locomotive superintendent of the B&DJ. Hudson chose the youngest, Matthew Kirtley, but not to keep the cost down—a rise of £50 a year to £250 went with the job. Hudson believed him to be the right man, a verdict amply justified by Kirtley's distinguished career, lasting until his death in 1873. Josiah Kersley took the appointment badly and required the company to buy out his contract.

The 1844 locomotive stock can only be described as inadequate; passenger traffic was rising, the Great Exhibition was looming, coal loadings were rising, and soon Kirtley's responsibilities would include the Bristol line with the added 'attraction' of the 1 in 37 Lickey Bank, a fierce proposition until the end of steam. Many of the locomotives were fit only for the breakers' yard, so in desperation Kirtley was authorised to enter into an arrangement with the Saltley firm of Henry Wright to hire ten locomotives with drivers, firemen and cleaners, at a cost of one shilling (£0.05) per mile, excluding coke.

For the daunting task of repairing motive power for the longest line in England, Kirtley had at his disposal the works of the three Derby companies at Derby and a small set of workshops at Holmes, near

Rotherham. None was set up to manufacture locomotives, only to repair them.

The foresight of the Derby Corporation had ensured that there would be room enough for the locomotive works at Derby. The facilities were basically good and Kirtley set about improving them. They became in time one of the great locomotive works of the world, competing in fame with Swindon, Crewe and Doncaster. When the Midland was combined with the LNWR at the Grouping in 1923 to form the London Midland & Scottish Railway, Derby became the locomotive headquarters of the largest joint stock railway in the world.

The idea of building locomotives was foreign to all early railways except the remarkable GWR, so a number of enterprising and competent makers had sprung up in the manufacturing districts of the North and Midlands to supply the needs of the booming railways. Repair shops were essential as the makers were unwilling to devote valuable shop space to repair work when they were inundated with new orders. Kirtley decided to concentrate on a few good makers, abandoning the Bury small engine idea following his own experience on the L&B before joining the Derby line. He favoured the 2-2-2 pattern for passenger work, buying 28 from Sharp Stewart, followed by a remarkable locomotive the *Jenny Lind* (named after a popular opera singer) from Wilson of Leeds. The chief designer of that company, David Joy, had noticed the successful running of a mixed-frame locomotive on the small Hull & Selby railway, in which the driving axle had inside bearings, leaving the leading and trailing axles on outside frames. Two inside cylinders drove 6ft 0in wheels, the cylinders being 20in stroke by 15in diameter. To allow for an inside firebox, the frames terminated at the front of the casing. These locomotives had the useful new Stephenson link motion invented at the drawing office of Robert Stephenson's company by the chief draughtsman, Mr Howe. Stephenson never called it the 'Stephenson' motion, but referred to it by the inventor's name. The key to the success of the 'Jennys' was in the high boiler pressure of 120lb/sq in—80lb/sq in was usual in the 1840s. Kirtley found that the 'Jennys' gave good service on the Midland. Many were built at Derby and by E. B. Wilson at Leeds over the next few years. The 'Jennys' characterised the early Kirtley years at Derby; one survived, much rebuilt, until the 1920s!

For goods work Kirtley held to the robust inside-cylinder 0-6-0 then slowly evolving into the great British standard goods locomotive. Many hundreds of 0-6-0s were built down the years all over the country—solid, dependable and hardworking, all basically going back to the Stephenson 'Long Boiler.' This seminal design evolved from a set of experiments made on the North Midland by Robert Stephenson, who suspended a series of cones of different metals inside the smokebox of one of his locomotives. Seeing which cones had melted gave a simple and elegant measure of the temperature of the smokebox gases. Horrified at the high temperatures—arising from the poor thermal efficiency of the locomotives, Stephenson produced a more efficient design having a longer boiler. The express versions were called 'Polkas' for their poor riding, but the goods long boiler 0-6-0s were a much better proposition.

Kirtley performed wonders—he had no money to play with. The improvidence of Hudson had left the Midland desperately short of money. How John Ellis retrenched and saved the very existence of the Midland comes later.

The Midland & Great Northern Joint Railway

The northern rural reaches of Norfolk were in the 1860s far from ideal country for railway building. Purely agricultural, sparsely populated, they could never generate enough traffic to sustain main lines. Nevertheless, a collection of single-track rural railways was built around King's Lynn, stretching to Cromer, a resort town on the Norfolk coast. Main line connections were made with the Great Northern Railway, north of Peterborough.

When financial problems forced amalgamation, the Eastern & Midland was formed out of several rural lines. This railway was soon short of cash and despite valiant efforts by its board, the line ended in Chancery—run by the courts.

In the early 1890s a plan to build a connection from Bourne to Saxby, on the Midland's Leicester to Peterborough line, led to Midland interest in the bankrupt railway. Wise counsels prevailed, and a joint takeover by the Midland & Great Northern followed in 1893, forming a delightful and much loved joint railway.

Run by a committee formed from the boards of the two owning companies (the chairman alternating MR or GN at successive meetings) the headquarters of the M&GNJR were at Melton Constable. The Midland, as with the S&D, provided locomotives, the GN looking after the permanent way. The joint manager and engineer, Mr Marriott, served the line faithfully for long years from his Melton

Constable offices, ruling a staff of dedicated rural railwaymen with a firm benevolent hand.

The long lengths of single tracks made for poor timekeeping, despite the use of automatic tablet changers. The safety record of this mainly single line was excellent, unmarred by any major accident. Services were slow, apart from the crack King's Cross to Cromer expresses and the well-loved cross-country trains from Leicester to Cromer. Johnson locomotives were much in evidence in all parts of the M&GN, interspersed with ancient tank engines from the pre E&M lines and a small number of workmanlike Melton Constable products.

The railway outlived the Midland, continuing beyond grouping to be run very much as before by the LMS and LNER. Post-war closures took their toll, leaving Melton Constable as a ghost town, where once plied Johnson 4-4-0s and sturdy engines. As with many loved railways, its memory is preserved on the steam-operated Sheringham Light Railway.

The Irish Connection

In 1903, seized by an expansionist mood, the Midland bought a complete railway track, locomotives, rolling stock, everything! The line brought into the Midland fold was the Belfast & Northern Counties, whose main line ran from Belfast to Londonderry, with a major branch to Larne. Regular sailings operated between Larne and Stranraer, meeting Glasgow boat trains of the G&SWR. A number of minor narrow gauge branches also came with the purchase, but the line to Derry dominated the NC&B traffic.

The Northern Counties was always a separate and distinct entity, with little mainland Midland flavour about it. Some of its features were strange to Midland eyes; signals were to the GN somersault pattern, and many locomotives, designed by the veteran engineer Bowman Malcolm, used the Von Borries two-cylinder compound design. Pioneered in the UK by T. W. Worsdell of the North Eastern Railway, its low coal usage was attractive in the province, where all coal was imported.

After grouping the line became known as the Northern Counties Committee of the LMS. By a strange chance the NCC took on a very Midland flavour under a new, vigorous general manager, Major Spiers. The rejuvenated line painted its locomotives dark red and smartened-up its services to Midland standards. The most important change was to straighten the line at Birtisland, where trains to Derry and Portrush had to reverse. A huge flying junction, built with funds used for job creation schemes, allowed first-rate timings for the first time since the line to Derry was built. Major Spiers, a Euston appointment, truly brought the Midland to life again in Northern Ireland, compounds and all!

Midland Marine

Since the early days of the 'Little North Western' and the associated Furness Railway line to Barrow, there had been a boat train service to Belfast from the port. By the end of the 19th Century the Midland, which was casting envious eyes at these services, built a new harbour at Heysham, served by a branch from the Morcambe Line. Less sensitive to tides than Morcambe itself, Heysham proved a winner and is still used by Sealink sailings.

A small fleet of fine steamers, two capable of 20 knots, plied from the new harbour to Belfast and to Douglas, Isle of Man.

A crack Irish boat train left St Pancras at 5.00pm, resplendent with the latest products of Litchurch Lane, calling at Kettering. Nottingham, Sheffield and Leeds, reaching Belfast at 6.00am the following morning. Another train left St Pancras at 8.00am for Douglas, gaining Heysham by 2.45pm for the three-hour crossing to Douglas in the powerful *Manxman*, pride of the fleet.

The events of 1914 dealt harshly with Douglas, which was left to the LNWR Fleetwood services and to the Isle of Man Steam Packet Company's Liverpool services. This situation was reversed in 1928 when the Ulster Express was transferred from Fleetwood to Heysham. Two trains served the crossing to Belfast, one from Euston, the other from St Pancras, which picked up traffic from its Midland and Yorkshire stops. Three fine steamers were introduced to coincide with this new Belfast service, *Duke of Lancaster*, *Duke of Argyll* and *Duke of Rothesay*. After World War II Heysham really came into its own with a Sealink service to Douglas using a comfortable car ferry to the Isle of Man. This excellent crossing is preferred by the author to the rival Liverpool services, despite the longer journey from London to Heysham.

4

COMPETITION AND RETRENCHMENT

The Wounded Line

Sunshine and showers, up and down again like snakes and ladders, were the expectations of shareholders in the Midland Railway in its first six years from 1844 to 1850. Victorian railways were run to make money for the shareholders, the 'proprietors', as they were called. In 1845 on the Midland they could look forward to seven percent on their investment; by 1850 this had dropped to only two percent, a very poor return by any standard. When John Ellis took over the Chairmanship of the line in 1849 from Hudson, who had defected to the GN camp, taking the Y&NM with him, the shareholders were calling for blood. The inevitable committee of enquiry had found no impropriety in the accounts despite a certain lack of distinction, common to mid-Victorian times, between capital and revenue. The longest line in Great Britain at 434 miles, with its two main routes from Leeds to Rugby and from Derby down to Bristol, it served rich coalfields and was close to the main centres of production in the Midlands and in Leeds. Unfortunately, the GN could tap the London trade and feed it right to the capital. All Midlands to London traffic went by the LNWR via the congested junction at Rugby. By 1849, the line was in trouble, but was rescued after a monumental struggle by John Ellis.

Hudson had left the Midland in a poor way; the legal costs of opposing the GN Bill were astronomical, too little had been spent on maintenance, while capital for the Lincoln and Peterborough branches was still being paid off.

A glance at the railway map of the early 1850s tells the tale; the total mileage of rails in England had doubled since 1840 and the Midland found itself hemmed in by rivals.

Above all, by 1850 the GN was tapping most of the passenger traffic from Scotland, Newcastle, Leeds and Sheffield areas. An accountant looking at the Midland's books in the late 1840s and early 1850s would have shaken his head and moved his savings to the GN or the GWR. From a respectable 49 per cent in 1845, the rate of return on total revenue had fallen by 1859 to a disastrous 13 per cent. In the same year the GWR was pulling in 60 per cent, rising to 65 per cent the following year. Even the added traffic brought by the Great Exhibition of 1851 could not save the day—much was carried down the GN direct to London, no changing at Rugby, waiting for an hour or more while LNWR took the congested road to London.

The GN was set to take most of the long-distance traffic, while the LNWR took over the Midland's passengers at Rugby. It was all the more sad that the Great Exhibition was not destined to generate a large flow of profitable passenger traffic. The Midland was closely associated with the architect of the Crystal Palace, Joseph Paxton, gardener to the Duke of Devonshire whose house Chatsworth is close to the Midland main line north of Ambergate. In the late 1840s Paxton became involved in the affairs of the railway, and during a visit to London for a consultation with John Ellis, learned that Parliament had rejected a large number of designs for the forthcoming exhibition. This set Paxton thinking and, the story goes, he designed the Crystal Palace on Midland blotting paper in dull intervals at a Derby board meeting. Sadly, the GN was opened in time to steal much of the expected extra London traffic.

The pages of Bradshaw tell us clearly why the GN was so favoured. Edmund Dennison, its architect had insisted on a direct line down from York and Hudson's defection to the GN camp had also ensured that the Leeds services via Doncaster and Knottingley were faster than on the Midland's longer line through Derby and Rugby. By 1857, the fastest train from London to Leeds, the 9.00am, took 5 hours 25 minutes using the Derby line, over 30 minutes slower than the GN train leaving King's Cross only 15 minutes later. Only an idiot would travel to York via Derby if time mattered. This was bad enough, but the GN Sheffield services really showed what the Doncaster company could do! In 1857 a new train to Manchester speeded via the GN, taking the sharp curve at Retford to the Manchester, Sheffield & Lincolnshire line to Sheffield Victoria and on to the cotton capital. This reached Sheffield in an astonishing 3 hours 40 minutes— the fastest Midland service was 5 hours 35 minutes via Derby. The competition was just too hot for Ellis and even cheap fares could not stem the GN victory. The author must confess that even today, when business takes him to Sheffield or Rotherham, the 08.00 HST, 'GN' to Doncaster, plus a lift from a kind colleague into Sheffield, takes some beating.

How then did the Midland weather the storms of the late 1840s? Competition could so easily have driven it into the welcoming but fatal arms of the ever-watchful, expanding LNWR, under its buccaneer of a general manager, Mark Huish. Instead the Midland survived, stabilised in the early 1850s and later grew from a provincial line into one of the big five English railways, rivalling the GWR in the luxury of its services. In the care and comfort of its passengers it had no rival, introducing the third class onto all its trains, giving the 'lower orders' access to rapid travel in decent conditions.

John Ellis nursed his ailing railway like a sick child, conserving its strength. No more expensive branches were laid. Only the useful Erewash Valley line from Nottingham, short and profitable, was built to tap the reserves of the rich Derbyshire coalfield and the newly-emerging Nottinghamshire concealed coal beds. Ellis took every advantage of the enormous growth of industrial production in the early 1850s. He fought tooth and nail to protect his growing mineral traffic from predatory neighbours, using both brute force and subtle diplomacy. He was also blessed with the good fortune that the GN was slow to exploit its freight traffic.

Recovery

The 1851 exhibition proved to be a turning point in the British economy; the heroic period of experimentation in new technology in the first half of the 19th Century was giving way to years of steady growth, interrupted only by depressions at intervals of ten years or thereabouts. Everything was growing, especially railways, coal and iron. All the graphs were to climb higher and higher, led by iron. Coal production, one-third of which was used in the iron industry, followed upward, especially in the East Midlands, saving the fortunes of the Midland. If we go back a hundred years to the 1750s, iron was still refined by charcoal in small furnaces making at most a few tons at a time. When the Darby family of Coalbrookdale near modern Telford discovered how to reduce the iron oxides to iron by using coke, a monumental change opened the way to large-scale iron production, released from the stranglehold of the dwindling supplies of charcoal.

That iron was still brittle and fit only for use in bridges where weight was not important, or pots, fireplaces and the like. Then in the 1790s, spurred on by Naval needs, an iron-maker named Cort working near Portsmouth found a way to make virtually pure iron by adding mill scale and by working the liquid iron by 'puddling.'

Rolling or forging the iron produced wrought iron. The age of modern engineering was born.

Wrought iron made the railways possible—the 80 lb/yd rails, strong enough to carry the bigger locomotives of the 1850s were all made of the material, usually from the great ironworks near Merthyr in South Wales. The locomotives themselves were made almost entirely of high grade iron, almost as strong as the steel which would replace it later in the century. Boiler pressures were rising, first to 100 lb/sq in then 150 lb/sq in and beyond, calling on the skills of the iron puddlers and boilersmiths alike.

The demand for iron after 1850 rose steadily in part because of the voracious needs of the railways built during the 'Mania.' Wrought iron needed vast quantities of coal for its production, so coalfields expanded, needing in turn extra lines to serve the growing colleries. A cycle of expansion grew in iron, coal and railway lines, which lasted until the end of the century.

The Midland was in the thick of this great growth of English Industry. The Nottingham coalfield along the Erewash produced an extra half million tons a year after 1850 compared with only 25,000 extra tons a year in the 1840s. Later the 'concealed' field over towards Mansfield and Worksop would add even more to the coal carried by the Midland.

Coal was the Midland Railway's saviour; the Great Northern was slow to exploit goods traffic and allowed the Midland to capitalise on the great boom. By 1860 the Midland carried 12 per cent of the country's minerals—not bad for a provincial line!

The ironworks in the Midland Railway's area were also growing, although not at the rate of the great works of South Wales or the Monklands in Scotland. Quality rather than quantity was the watchword for the ironworks of the Erewash Valley. Two great firms had started iron making nearby Derby, both to stay in the forefront of quality for two hundred years. The Butterley Company at Ripley rolled the sections used to make the London terminus of the Midland Railway, and remains to this day a force in quality engineering. A few miles away the Stanton blast furnaces made iron water pipes until recently, so that the words 'Stanton & Staveley' are buried beneath many of the roads of Britain.

These two great trades coal and iron grew to save the Midland so that by the mid-1850s John Ellis could pass on the reins of the chairmanship confident that the dividends, once more above £3.00 a share, would soon double to reach and surpass £6.00 a share.

Still, the battle to save the Midland was not won easily. War with the GN was fought on two fronts, one real and physical, the other veiled in the courts, in Parliament and in the office of a curious ally, Mark Huish of the LNWR. The physical battle took place in the heartland of the Midland, in Nottingham. It could not happen today so let us see how the Victorians reacted to competition!

The Battle of Nottingham

This direct and very physical battle is almost inconceivable in these days of slow official action. The Victorian took a more down-to-earth view of rivalry and was not afraid of a bit of force if his patch was threatened. The 'Battle of Nottingham' started with the 'Mania' and the desire of the Nottingham City fathers to end their town's branch line status, from Midland Counties days. After the usual committee and a couple of false starts a line was built from Grantham on the GN to Colwick, just to the east of Nottingham. There a junction led to the Midland line and by running powers into the Midland's large Nottingham station. The name of this independent line was over-ambitious—Ambergate, Nottingham, Boston & Eastern Junction Railway (called 'the Ambergate' for the rest of this book). Opened in 1851 it was wooed by both the Midland and the GN. Services were sparse, but a London connection to King's Cross would have taken even more traffic away from the Derby route. The first attempt at a takeover by the Midland was foiled by a shrewd and wealthy GN shareholder who bought a 'corner' in Ambergate shares. Round One to the GN! A near amalgamation with the GN followed, but Ellis was a match for them and caused a disaffected shareholder to secure an Order in Chancery prohibiting the GN from running into Nottingham. Round Two to the MR! Shortly before the GN opened its direct 'Towns' line to the North in 1881 the company advertised a Nottingham service (ignoring the legal niceties), quicker than the Derby, Rugby roundabout. On 1 August 1852 the first GN train ran into Nottingham, carrying a few luckless passengers, followed and preceded by Midland locomotives. A contest described as 'elephantine' took place—the lonely GN locomotive was incarcerated in an old shed, unable to leave as the rails in front of the interloper had been pulled up! Round Three and first match to the Midland.

The next conflict moved the contestants to the courts, smoke-filled committee rooms at Derby, Euston, and to the clubs of St James'. No blows were exchanged, but words were deep and cutting.

The Smoke-filled Rooms

The Great Northern managed to open its superb direct line from Leeds and York to London in time to attract most of the huge 1851 Exhibition traffic away from the Midland and the London & North Western, which carried London-bound passengers south of Rugby. The Midland and the LNWR cut fares, the GN followed, and so on until the excursion fare from the Victorian equivalent of a 'bucket shop' was only five shillings (£0.25) from Leeds.

At this stage entered an amazing character worthy of the most far-fetched television oil-family saga. Mark Huish was the secretary of the Grand Junction, retaining that post when the LNWR was formed. He ran the North Western in a highly professional way, combining managerial skills with cunning diplomacy amounting to genius. He had no scruples at all. The secretary of the GN, Seymore Clarke, was like a child in comparison; even though he was a first-class railwayman, at home with the nuts and bolts of railway operation, he was a child in the world of company intrigue. The LNWR was beset by competition on all sides, with the GWR attacking its right flank and the GN its left. Huish reacted by forming the 'Euston Square Confederacy,' an association of lines of which the LNWR, the Midland, and the Manchester, Sheffield & Lincolnshire were the most notable. Their aim, led by Huish, was to combine to protect their interests against competition from the GN and the GW. Seeing that the Midland's fortunes were at a low ebb, Huish at first proposed an amalgamation with the Midland. Terms were discussed, but Ellis held out for a fair price. Later, a second attempted amalgamation was foiled by Parliament, suspicious of any hint of a monopoly.

Huish then led a consortium of lines threatened by the GN in an agreement with the GN to limit the damage caused by the new fast East Coast route. Covering traffic between London and Scotland, eight companies were involved, working three routes:

Euston to Edinburgh via the LNWR to Preston, then by the Lancaster & Carlisle to the Border and the Caledonian to Edinburgh.

Euston to Rugby, LNWR; MR to Normanton; YNM to York; YN&B to Berwick, and on to Edinburgh via the North British Railway.

GN to Lincoln and Knottingley, later via Grantham; YNM to York; YN&B to Berwick, and NB to Edinburgh.

Under the 'octuple' agreement, passenger traffic was equally divided between the East and West coast routes, and the East coast share was split:

for passengers	GN/YNM	63%
	LNWR/MR	37%
for goods	GN/YNM	50%
	LNWR/MR	50%

This 1851 agreement which guaranteed the Midland recompense if the GN route proved to be too attractive to passengers, was a life-saver. A similar arrangement covered traffic between stations outside London, Edinburgh and Glasgow, and was called the 'sextuple' to differentiate it from the main 'octuple' agreement.

Credit for this master stroke must go to Huish, who hit the GN before its first 'Towns Route' was opened and before even Dennison, the GN Chairman, realised how attractive would be his new fast line, and how good would be its trains powered by the Swindon inspired express locomotives designed by Archibald Sturrock.

Another life-saver resulted from the fierce rate cutting of 1851. Gladstone, the Government minister responsible for railways, made a traffic-sharing award between the MR and GN for trains between London and the Northern towns of Leeds, Sheffield, Wakefield, York, Doncaster and Lincoln. This secured the greater share of the growing Sheffield and Leeds goods traffic to the Derby route. Some passenger receipts were even gained from the Yorkshire towns, no matter how slow the Midland was in getting to London by its tortuous and outmoded line.

Huish dominated the meetings of the committees formed to watch over these agreement and awards. Even in the late 1850s when the GN management realised the strength of its negotiating hand, Huish wrangled renewal of those agreements which so favoured the LNWR. His victories were also at some cost to the Midland, which had rented the 'Little North Western.' This had opened-up the possibility of the Midland running Anglo-Scottish trains via Derby and the 'Little North Western' to Carlisle and beyond.

Huish had also driven too hard a bargain with the Midland as a price for the life-saving GN arrangement, involving a 'common purse' fund for all receipts. The Midland, recovering in the late 1850s, tried to remove the shackles of its ally the LNWR, and even an amalgamation with its arch-enemy the GN was mooted at one point. Eventually Huish destroyed himself by his own tortuous web of arrangements, made with utter disregard for his allies.

Huish went unmourned, especially by men like McConnel, once the locomotive superintendent of the Birmingham & Gloucester, later sacked from the same job on the Southern Section on the LNWR.

By this time the Midland was strong enough, built up by its growing mineral traffic, to contemplate removing the incubus of its junction with the LNWR at Rugby. Passenger delays at Rugby were a standing joke and delays to mineral trains were reaching disaster proportions. Something had to be done—read on to find the answers to Ellis' problems.

5

CONSOLIDATION

The Midland Breathes Again

At length after the terrible early 1850s John Ellis could see his way through. The Midland Railway had survived the twin threats of the Great Northern and Mark Huish, the latter sitting spider-like at Euston. The Midland belt had been drawn in, overheads cut to the bone, wonders performed by the operating staff, and the Midland cashed in on the extraordinary growth in the coal and steel trades of the early 1850s.

By 1853 Ellis saw that to fend off the GN and the LNWR, the Midland needed to become a national line. Gone were the days when it was sufficient to carry coal around the Midlands. The line needed to fight its way out to the south and to London, to strike north-west to the rich markets of Lancashire, and to reach Scotland. Ellis took two great steps. The first was to appoint a professional general manager, James Allport; the second was to start the drive to London—a drive which occupied Allport's energies for the rest of the decade.

Closer to London

Even though the London & North Western Railway put down a third line to help take the enormous volume of traffic running to London, goods and passenger alike, from Rugby, the congestion was becoming too much for the Midland. Naturally, the North Western traffic took the road whenever a Midland load competed for the right of way. As London grew, so did the demand for coals, and traffic reached saturation point on the North Western at Rugby. Telegraph messages from that time reading 'Stop all coals from Butterley Colliery for Acton, Hammersmith and Kew, for three days, as Willesden Sidings are blocked up' or 'Rugby is blocked so as not to be able to shunt any

Midland Stations – Derby: Derby, the pivot of the Midland systems, remained the headquarters of the line until Grouping in 1923. The superb NMR station, designed by Thompson, was the first of many main line stations in the Midlands and the North designed on classical lines. It never recovered properly from wartime bombing and is now being redeveloped. This early print shows the station as built, before the *porte-cochère* was added. *Derby Local Interest Library.*

Midland Station – Kettering: This fine example of a 'High Midland' intermediate station, extensively rebuilt in the 1890s, has rich glass canopies over each platform with characteristic Midland cast-iron decorated supports. Once deemed to be far from London, the hourly InterCity 125s have brought it within one hour of West End offices. the 'house style' is BR London Midland Region, but the station name was displayed on a four-sided lozenge shaped board for greater visibility.

more' were common. The Midland directorate revived a scheme granted an Act in the 1847-8 session, to build a line from Leicester, through Northamptonshire, to Hitchin on the Great Northern main line. Dropped at the time for lack of funds and because of the intense ill-feeling between the two companies, it was revived and re-submitted to Parliament in 1853. In this instance there was no opposition from landowners; one Samuel Whitbread felt so strongly in favour of the line that he sold land to the Midland amounting to one eighth of the total, at the agricultural value of £80 an acre. The Midland shareholders were also pleased to be reminded of the vast mineral wealth of the Northamptonshire ironstone fields crossed by the line to Hitchin.

Support for the Hitchin line was given by the citizens of Bedford, who saw an end to their dependence on the slow LNWR branch from Bletchley. Small wonder that Parliament readily passed the new Hitchin line Bill.

Leaving the Leicester to Rugby line near the then small village of Wigston, the new line swung round by a sharp curve toward Market Harborough, then over a summit near Desborough and down into Kettering. A few miles further it reached the ancient leatherworking town of Wellingborough, later to become a famous 'Midland' centre, with extensive sheds and a works second only to Derby. A short branch to the LNWR line from Northampton to Peterborough left the main line near Wellingborough, before it swept on towards London, over the Wellingborough viaduct, the only major work on this line. Bedford was gained after a few more miles of reasonably easy country, followed by the last easy short run to Hitchin and a junction with the GN, dropping down into King's Cross. Hitchin was only 32 miles short of London, bringing the Midland 50 miles closer to its long-term objective. Opened in 1858, the Hitchin route relieved traffic, although the Midland still sent a good proportion of its London-bound coal trains via Rugby as GN tariffs were high for that traffic.

Relieving the pressure from the LNWR, the line proved to be an effective stop-gap until the Midland had its own 'London Extension.' With reasonable gradients and well laid out curves, the Wigston to Bedford portion is now the main line to Leicester. With track made up to HST 125 requirements, it is one of Britain's major InterCity routes. The effect on the County of Northampton was dramatic. Kettering was a decayed market centre, with half its population on poor relief. The railway changed all that, bringing back prosperity to the leather trade.

Estimated to cost close on £1,000,000 by its engineer, Charles Liddell, construction started in 1854, with most work let to the great contractor, Thomas Brassey. Although not passing through really difficult country, substantial earthworks were needed as the line crossed three river valleys. Going south, the Welland was crossed near Market Harborough, then the Nene at Wellingborough and the Great Ouse at Bedford. Planned originally with a modest ruling gradient, the events of the Crimean War (when Brassey was called upon to support the British troops with a small army of 'navigators') required a drastic reappraisal of the extensive earthworks. The result was a switchback with gradients in the region of 1 in 100 near to Desborough, Kibworth and Sharnbrook, posing problems for locomotive departments until modern times. In all 18 stations were built, most in a pleasant 'cottage style.' Only those at Market Harborough, Wellingborough, and Kettering now remain to show the Midland's famous glass roofs, which may well have owed something to Paxton, the builder of the Crystal Palace and a Midland board member.

The site of Bedford station was discussed with the LNWR which already had a station on its branch from Bletchley. Would it be that for once in Victorian times a joint, sensible station would emerge? Not so. After long and detailed negotiations Bedford was destined to have two stations, until the 1980s. What was worse, to keep costs down the two lines crossed on the level, always a bad arrangement, leading in this case to a fatal accident a few years later.

Building the line was delayed by every imaginable cause. The navigators left the works to reap the harvest, the wet weather caused serious slippages of embankments and even of stone viaducts, the many accidents (nine of them fatal) held up the work until the engineer was under pressure from the directors to speed progress. The last straw was the death of Horne, the resident engineer. Brassey dispatched his brother-in-law to take charge.

The section between Sharnbrook and Irchester which now looks so solid and complete was a sore trial, with the massive embankments and cuttings delayed time and time again. The modern traveller should remember as he speeds along the thousands of navvies who worked on this stretch by night in poor lighting as well as by day.

7 May 1857 saw the opening from an enlarged Leicester, London Road, station by the usual special train to Bedford and Hitchin. The Mayor of Bedford had most to celebrate; his town was now properly on the railway map. At first a relief route to the Rugby route, journey times to Leicester were similar and the bulk of the passenger traffic continued to use the older services. Through carriages were available

via Rugby, while the GN cannily required all passengers to change onto its own trains at Hitchin. The timetables reflect this difference, with eight trains a day each way to Leicester via Rugby and four via Hitchin. Even goods continued to pour onto the LNWR, as the GN kept its tariffs high to ensure that the Midland did not get too much of a foothold in King's Cross.

The new line did in fact act as a safety valve for the LNWR route to London. Equally important, it served to keep the GN away from the lucrative Leicester area. However, Denison was still in charge at Doncaster; he well remembered the alliances with Huish of the North Western and their damaging effects on the infant GN. The Midland was tolerated at Hitchin because Parliament had so decreed, but King's Cross was definitely out of bounds.

The Midland at King's Cross

The celebrations attending the opening of the Midland's new main line to Hitchin were muted by the Great Northern ruling that all trains from Bedford were to stop at Hitchin and all their passengers were to re-book within the two or three minutes allowed for connections. Then the Midland general manager, Allport, persisting with his negotiations to gain running powers to King's Cross, eventually struck a hard bargain with Dennison for a seven-year period giving the GN a guaranteed £20,000 a year. In return the GN built a small locomotive shed at King's Cross and undertook to give the Midland trains free and reasonable access to the London terminus.

Things worked out well at first, the Midland even going as far as building a new large station at Bedford to avoid the awkward reversing into the LNWR station, much disapproved of by the Inspectors of Railways. Even though much of the traffic still went via the old route through Rugby, pressure grew on the King's Cross route like a boiler with a screwed-down safety valve.

The Midland in 1860 was a company full of boundless confidence that its policy was exansionist and aggressive in the extreme! The country's economy was growing apace. By a combination of growth in all the trades, coal, iron, and not the least important to the Midland's fortunes, Burton beer, with the aggression of the company's agents, the goods traffic more than doubled between 1852 and 1859. That was not all; the coal trade to London was being taken from the coastal ships by the efforts of the Midland and its goods agents. Between 1852 and 1859 mineral traffic expanded more than three-fold, passenger trains flowed in increasing numbers with London, overloading the line, reducing safety.

As the heavy, poorly-braked trains would take half-a-mile or more to stop even when going at only a few miles an hour along the over loaded tracks, the 1862 season was soon marred by two particularly bad accidents. In one case the excursion traffic was heavy, so return- ing trains to the Midlands were divided into Leicester and Burton sections. Both halves carried over 500 passengers and left King's Cross only five minutes apart. Staff were not informed in advance about the second train, a white light on the tail of the main half serving as the only indication. The Sharnbrook bank out of Bedford proved to be a trial until the last days of steam, so it was small wonder that the first locomotive stopped at Bedford to take on water. The second also stopped, keeping the gap between trains to a barely safe five minutes. All was not well with the leading train, which was forced to halt at Market Harborough to top up with water after the fierce Desborough bank. Hearing the second train coming in the quiet night the driver tried desperately to move ahead. Couplings snapped under the strain, the second portion piled into the stranded carriages, causing one death and nearly thirty serious injuries. Reading of this tragedy, caused by a complete absence of safety measures, the modern traveller must wonder how the growing rail traffic of the 1860s was carried without wholesale slaughter.

The overloaded lines were blocked by never-ending processions of MR trains on the four tracks into King's Cross. GN trains always took precedence, so the poor Midland passengers suffered endless delays, often within sight of their journeys' end.

By 1862 enough was enough; despite overtures from the GN, which now found that it enjoyed a £36,000 annual fee for the Hitchin traffic, the Midland obtained an Act for a direct line from Bedford to London.

The London Extension

October 1962 was a momentous month for the Midland. At the board meeting on the 14th the railway decided to throw off its provincial shackles and become a national line with a terminus in the Capital, striking south from Bedford on the Leicester to Hitchin line to a terminus near King's Cross.

Railways approaching London from the north had three obstacles to overcome, two natural, the third man-made. The Chilterns thrusting north-west across the path of lines trying to reach London from the Midlands, and Hampstead Hill acted as natural barriers in the path of London-bound lines. The man-made hurdle was put up, sensibly, by Parliament to bring some semblance of order into the rash of railway terminals built in 19th Century London. The Royal Commission on Railway Termini within the Metropolis had ruled that on the north side of the Thames no new railway should intrude into an area bounded by the New Road (now the Euston Road), Edgware Road, Marylebone Road, Pentonville Road and a ring of roads defining the eastern and western edges of an inviolate central area.

This set a southern limit to the Midland Railway's approach to London, however much the directors would have liked to have penetrated to the City or the West End. They settled for a terminus on the Euston Road near their goods depot, built in the odoriferous slums of Agar Town, next to their rivals at King's Cross.

The Midland's proposed London extension left what was now the Hitchin branch just south of Bedford and crossed the easy Bedfordshire countryside to Ampthill, making for the gap through the Chilterns near Luton, then a medium-size manufacturing town known for its straw hats. South of Luton, the Midland put the ancient cathedral city of St Albans on its main line. A short tunnel at Elstree led into the then rural villages of Mill Hill and Hendon and so on to Cricklewood, where the Midland built large goods concentration yards and a locomotive depot. An important branch turned off towards the south-west to meet the imposing-sounding North & South West Junction Railway, to join the London & South Western at Kew Bridge, giving an outlet to the south-west for the burgeoning coal trade aggressively expanded by the Midland in the 1860s.

At this stage the line ran well to the west of the Hampstead Hills, close to the Roman road to St Albans. As the Midland already had extensive goods facilities near to King's Cross it made sense to build new passenger and goods terminals in that district. Thus the line swung around the foot of the Hampstead Hills, through a long tunnel at Belsize Park, before turning south towards a new terminus at the Euston Road and a junction with the Metropolitan Railway, newly built beneath London's streets from Paddington to the City.

Engineering supervision was shared between two men, Charles Liddle and the Midland's consulting engineer, William Barlow, an unusual arrangement which seems to have worked well.

The work was let in eight contracts, with the usual problems—a failed contractor, navvies deserting the works at harvest time, and the depredations of a series of wet summers. A new problem rose in 1866 when the bankers Overend & Gurney collapsed, leaving the money markets in a state of acute jitters and several railways in a bankrupt condition. Work was pressed ahead in 1867 as fast as possible to avoid a complete withdrawal of funds by investors. Four tracks were laid to Hendon, except in the Belsize Tunnel. Despite landowners holding on to land illegally and (surprisingly) a great shortage of bricks throughout constructions, the line was opened on time in the Agar Town goods terminal in September 1867.

St Pancras Station

Then this workaday line was transformed by the almost magical addition of a great railway terminus, built in keeping with the Midland's new image. St Pancras, designed by Barlow, the MR Engineer, was a masterpiece, complemented by a first-class hotel built in high Victorian Gothic style, easily outshone the confused and gimcrack Euston and drab King's Cross. St Pancras set the Midland tone of solid, dependable opulence.

Barlow, writing in the *Journal* of the Institution of Civil Engineers has given us an insight into the thinking that lay behind the magnificently roofed station as we see it today.

First, he had to build the railway over the Regent's Canal—an under-bridge would have meant too steep a gradient up to the Belsize tunnel and the Hampstead Heights. This in turn led him to plan a station some 12ft above the Euston Road. Set to build a massive earth embankment, Barlow's mind was jogged by the shrewd General Manager, Allport, who said, 'why not build over a cellar—just right for storing all those thousands of barrels of Burton ale we ship down each week for the thirsty Londoners'. Thus was the magnificent design set—all based on the size of a beer barrel!

Barlow then designed his magnificent station from the cellar upwards. So that the laden drays could move easily in and out, the cellar was level with the Euston Road. It was roofed with special buckled plates resting on cross-girders, the station floor supported by 720 cast-iron columns, spaced to pack in the maxiumum number of standard barrels.

Barlow reckoned that this rigid floor could be the lower tie for a great arched roof. Such a roof would at one stroke avoid driving columns down through the planned underground lines to the Metropolitan and allow flexibility of design in the station. It was designed with 24 great main ribs and a gable at the 'country' end; each rib,

costing just over £1,000, was erected using a vast wooden frame, moved along rails an inch at a time. This roof was matched at the Euston Road end by a wood panel booking hall worthy of an Oxford College, placed conveniently between the cab entrance and the platforms. The two arrival tracks were placed either side of a cab road and five other platforms were provided for departures and suburban services. The roof was 240ft wide, 689ft in length, and over 100ft high at its apex.

The strength of the roof, made by the Butterley Company, was well tested before completion of the whole station. A chronic shortage of bricks meant that the side walls were left unfinished for some time after the roof was finished, with no gale damage to the roof.

The whole station opened early in October 1868 without ceremony. The Midland had at last become a national railway with a terminus in the capital.

The Midland Hotel, built in the high Gothic style by Gilbert Scott, was a fitting frontage to the Barlow roof. Managed to the highest international standard, the hotel was praised by Baedeker's *Guide*, and well compared with the Ritz. Sadly, the hotel did not keep up with modern trends and closed in 1935. The hotel was one of the finest in the world, run by the former manager of the Victoria Hotel in Venice, equipped with every luxury, even to a telephone system for listening to live concert performances! Inside, the whole structure was a showpiece lovingly created by Gilbert Scott, who had been frustrated by failing to win the competition for the Foreign Office building. Built on the most lavish scale, the great staircase is a masterpiece of Victorian decorative art.

Mistaken it was said for a church by an American visitor, St Pancras remains a most impressive building. Alan Jackson described it in his *London Termini* as 'a worthy temple to the steam train. With its fine soaring Gothic towers, seen best from the Pentonville Road on a murky afternoon, it is indeed too hard to imagine that anything as prosaic as a railway station lies behind.' In steam days the great train

Midland Stations – St Pancras: (*top*) This fine photographs shows St Pancras shortly after building. The Midland Hotel, built in 'High Gothic' by Sir Charles Gilbert Scott, still delights the eye. Although threatened by demolition in the 1960s, improvements will soon be made to this elegant, stately station bringing it up to the highest modern standards of comfort. The hotel remains empty, but is to be restored to use. *National Building Archives*

(*below*) Taken on a fine cold winter morning, the sun shines in through the open end of the Barlow's great roof, each rib proudly proclaiming 'Made by the Butterley Co., 1876' at its base. The diesel-hauled train is the replacement for the 09.15 Nottingham train, usually an HST 125 set. *Author.*

shed reverberated to the sound of small sturdy tank engines pulling in rakes of Midland-like LMS coaches, decked out in a close relative to crimson lake. Trains to Scotland and the Midlands moved slowly out of the station at regular intervals, past the gasometers, through the grim tunnels, past Kentish town, pulled by Midland-like 4-4-0s or by Stanier Jubilees, worthy successors to the Kirtley 2-4-0s and the beautiful Johnson 'Spinners.'

St Pancras, whose nearby church is dedicated to a boy martyr in Asia Minor killed for his faith by the Emperor Diocletian, remains the best of London's termini. It avoids the frantic bustle of Charing Cross, the impersonal airport style of the new Euston, the chaos of Liverpool Street, the infinite walk across a never-ending concourse of Waterloo, the inconvenience of Paddington's arrangements of offices, and the crowding of King's Cross—a truly gracious station with friendly staff, clean, fast trains and the best beer in London.

The St Pancras Branch

In 1850 the centre of London was at the Mansion House not as it is said now, Piccadilly Circus. Many a traveller arriving at Paddington or even Euston would find himself at the start of a long and tedious journey through streets choked with every kind of transport before reaching his City destination. The Royal Commission of 1846 had prohibited any lines or stations between Hyde Park and the eastern edge of the City, also between the New Road and the River Thames. One way remained—to build under the streets. In 1850 a revolutionary new railway under the New Road was mooted. The North Metropolitan Railway, soon to drop the word 'North' from its title, was built from Paddington to King's Cross. A complementary underground line from King's Cross to Farringdon had been dropped through lack of finance, so the Metropolitan extended its line to Farringdon Street and beyond to serve the main Post Office. Money was slow to come in, the Crimean War did not help, but the Metropolitan was opened as far as Farringdon and Moorgate in 1863. The Underground then served London as it still does, slow, but invaluable. The Midland saw the advantage of a link with the Metropolitan to take its trains into Moorgate.

At first the Government Inspector had turned down the sharp curves and the punishing gradients of Barlow's first plans. Later he approved a proposal for the St Pancras branch, leaving the main line near Camden Road station, doubling under the terminus before swinging round under the front of the hotel to join the 'Widened Lines', an extra pair of Metropolitan lines built to take the extra traffic from a cross-London link forged between South London and the Metropolitan via Ludgate Hill. The London Chatham & Dover Railway, even in its impoverishment, had found enough capital to ruin the view of Saint Paul's Cathedral from Fleet Street, building one of the most intensively used railways in the world.

The St Pancras branch was easy to propose but difficult to build. The local authority with which the Midland had to treat was the Vestry of St Pancras, the ancient parish church lying close to the North London line. A breakout by the Fleet sewer at the building of the City Widened Lines had made the Vestry cautious of railway engineers, so a bond of £15,000 was needed before work could start. The other obstacle was the old church burial ground, long filled and abandoned.

Building the main line bridge over the old cemetery was bad enough, with elaborate precautions taken to avoid disturbance to the graves. Bones could only be disturbed on the written authority of Barlow himself. It had been estimated that the branch down to the Metropolitan would pass under the graveyard, but not so—the burial ground was so old that graves were found at great depths and there was no getting away from disturbing some. Large numbers of mouldering coffins were taken away for re-internment at St Pancras workhouse. An outbreak of cholera in the festering slums being destroyed (with no recompense or re-housing) in Agar Town and Somers Town made life even more wretched. The Fleet river passed through Somers Town, carrying all its filth down to the Thames. The Metropolitan Board of Works took advantage of the general disruption in the area to insist that the Fleet be enclosed, markedly reducing the spread of infections. Eventually all the work was done and the Midland was able to start sending trains down the City Widened Lines to Moorgate, and through Snow Hill to the LCDR system south of the Thames. In the days before the deep tube lines these cross-London links were invaluable; about 200 trains a day ran from the Midland and the GN into Moorgate, 100 a day going across the Thames to the Chatham Line.

The City Widened Lines were the epitome of the smoky pre-electric surface London links before World War I. Daily traffic patterns tell their story. Early morning saw roughly dressed manual workers taking advantage of cheap tickets to travel from their small crowded houses in Lambeth or near the Surrey docks to work on the new buildings in the Northern Heights. Later, bowler-hatted City clerks travelled from Lower Hampstead or Camden Road to their 'billets' in the City. Mid-morning saw grandmas venturing out to visit married daughters across the river in the new smart streets of Clapham or Balham, or shopping with new-found wealth in the shops of the Tottenham Court Road.

Bigger and yet Bigger

The 1860s were a time of continual expansion for the Midland. London was reached, then the great town of Manchester, the port of Liverpool, even furthest industrial West Wales was on the growing giant network of Midland lines. In 1860 the Midland was a provincial railway, serving Leeds, Derby and the Midlands—by 1870 it was a national British railway, well on the way to a leading position in the annals of railway history in the United Kingdom. The rest of this chapter tells how this great expansion was achieved.

The Lure of Manchester

It had not escaped the Derby board of directors that the great manufacturing city of Manchester was only 60 miles to the north-west of their headquarters. It was equally apparent to them that the country between Derby and Manchester was hostile in the extreme to the railways, for the Peaks lie right in the way of any railway striking from Derby to the north-west. Their foothills are pleasant, occupied by a number of stately homes, topped by the magnificent Chatsworth House where its owner, the Duke of Devonshire was an active supporter of Midland Railway development in the middle and late 19th Century. The Peaks though are a different matter, rising gradually up to the massive Kinder Scout. Any railway to Manchester and its rich trade in cotton and manufactured goods would have to climb over watersheds nearly 1,000ft high.

The Cromford & High Peak Railway line wandered from the Cromford Canal to the limestone quarries near Buxton and on to Whaley Bridge, following the contours of the hills, using inclined planes to gain height out of the valleys. The C&HP never came within a mile of being a main line railway. A small company with a long name but little money next took up the challenge. The Manchester, Buxton, Matlock & Midland Junction Railway (referred to here as the Ambergate line) made a start, backed by the young Midland Railway and the London & Birmingham, then looking for access to Manchester. The required capital of £3 million was not forthcoming despite the support of the Cavendish interests at Chatsworth. Opposition came from the Manchester, Sheffield & Ashton-under-Lyne Railway, which planned to build a line out of Manchester up towards the Peaks to the small mill town of Whaley Bridge. The company was bought off and authority came for the Ambergate to build a branch from the Midland up the Derwent Valley as far as Rowsley. The hopes of the Ambergate soon were shattered by the amalgamation of the L&B with the Grand Junction into the LNWR, giving the L&B interests direct and easy access to Manchester across the Cheshire Plain. The Ambergate continued to be dominated by the two major lines, the LNWR keeping a close eye on possible Midland moves over the Peaks.

The Midland eventually bought out the joint lease of the Ambergate, but not until the LNWR had throttled any attempt by the Ambergate to drive over the hills to Manchester. Unable to use its interest in the Ambergate to advantage, the Midland was forced to make a direct attempt on the Peaks and gain a route to Manchester on its own. Thwarted by the Duke of Devonshire who, not unreasonably, did not wish the rails to go right across his magnificent park at Chatsworth, the 'Peaks' line went up the Wye Valley. Leaving the Ambergate just short of its terminus at Rowsley, the Midland forced a way up the narrow gorges of the Wye through country of towering majesty. The first station up the line was at Bakewell, the Midland providing a station worthy of the occupants of nearby Haddon Hall. A tunnel built at the cost of several lives was driven near to Haddon just to preserve its view! That friend of the Midland, The Duke of Devonshire, used the next station along the line at Hassop. This too was much grander than the usual run of country stations. We must be grateful for the local worthies' interests which have left us with a fine legacy of sadly now disused stations along this stretch of the old Midland.

Beyond Bakewell the line was thrust using every trick of the Alpine railway engineer's art, through a series of gorges, Monsal Dale, Miller's Dale and Chee Dale. The beauty of Monsal Dale was enhanced by a superb viaduct, possibly the finest built by the Midland. The station in this remote valley opened up the Dales to generations of walkers escaping from the smoke of the industrial cities of Manchester and Sheffield. Miller's Dale station served as a junction for the branch to Buxton, a spa town situated high on the Peaks, unable to take advantage of a through route to Manchester on the Midland. The LNWR served it better, and the Manchester–Buxton services on the former North Western line still run. After Miller's Dale the line climbed up to the summit at Dove Holes, 1,000ft above sea level. Gradients were severe, with 1 in 90 being normal for the last few miles to the Dove Holes tunnel. From Peak Forest, known locally as 'Dove Oles' station, the line fell to the windswept quarry town of Chapel-en-le-Frith, where snow is not unknown in June.

The Midland managed to get as far as New Mills, a small cotton town in the foothills of the Peak District, and only 12 miles from Manchester, where it was stopped by the concerted efforts of the LNWR and the MS&L. Frustrated by these allies, the Midland Chairman and General Manager took themselves off armed with maps to view possible routes down the valleys from New Mills to the industrial plain. By chance, they met a director of the MS&L who was also looking over the country with a view to an extension of its system up towards New Mills and the traffic of the minor cotton towns nearby. Allport, who had also been the General Manager of the 'Money Sunk and Lost', knew their directors well. After a day spent looking over the land together it was agreed informally that the MS&L would build a Manchester to New Mills line via Marple, with running powers into the cotton capital for the Midland. This chance meeting opened up Manchester expresses on the Midland.

Trains to Manchester

The Midland Railway's early London to Manchester trains were no scorchers, taking a leisurely five hours, their small locomotives struggling double-headed over the Peak line. These timings were no worse than the lethargic LNWR, which did not believe in wasting money on fast trains. The Midland at first took a roundabout route down into Manchester from New Mills, going on the MS&L line via Hyde and on into the London Road terminus, shared by the MS&L and the LNWR. In 1875 a joint Midland and MS&L line was opened from Romily, across the bleak south-east Manchester manufacturing district into London Road, greatly shortening the run into the terminus. No sooner had the Midland settled down to using the shorter line and a new large goods depot at Ancoats than it was given notice to quit London Road. Fortunately the Cheshire Lines Committee, a joint Midland and MS&L system serving the south Manchester suburbs, had just opened a grand new terminal called Central just to the west of the city centre. In 1881 the Midland further improved the route into Manchester by a cut-off from Bredbury (on the Romily to Ashburys line), to Throstle Nest Junction just outside the new Central Station.

By 1883 train timings were smart, one express leaving Manchester at 3.45pm arriving in St Pancras at 8.20—not bad for the 1880s. By 1903 these times had improved to a basic four-hour service via the Peak Line, matching the MS&L services through Retford and the LNWR through Crewe.

The Midland also gave a lot of attention to Liverpool services, with smart timings on the popular boat trains. In 1880 an expensive cut-off was built from New Mills, through the Disley Tunnel, to Heaton Mersey, where trains could follow the Cheshire Lines Committee route to Liverpool or turn north to Manchester Central.

Local passenger traffic was never good. Even though the old Midland stations were usually well sited, the Buxton trains into Stockport, Tiviot Dale and Manchester Central could never compete with those on the old LNWR line through Stockport Edgeley to London Road, later Piccadilly. By the 1950s Buxton trains had become dirty, irregular, and ill-used.

The Peaks route came into its own in the early 1960s for long-distance services when the LNWR line was being electrified. St Pancras became the main London station for Manchester, with smart services to match. The Midland Pullman left Manchester Central at 8.50am, reaching St Pancras in just under four hours. After electrification of the West Coast Main Line, the curves and gradient across the Peaks were just 'too much' and the newly-electrified West Coast Main Line won hands down, leading to closure between Rowsley and Miller's Dale in 1967. The cruel gradients of the old LNWR line to Buxton left the old Midland line to Buxton via Miller's Dale and Dove Holes safe for limestone trains. Passenger services stayed on the LNWR line and the infinite calm of Stockport (Tiviot Dale) was broken by passenger trains no more.

While the Western Giant Slept

Coal production in South Wales exploded in the second half of the 19th Century to such an extent that the Midland Railway and the LNWR cast greedy eyes at the enormous and lucrative trade in Welsh coal. It did not escape the keen business sense of the Midland board that the coal carrier *par excellence*, the Taff Vale Railway, was the most profitable of all British railways, with no less than 6s 10$\frac{1}{2}$d (£0.34) earned per train mile and as little as 48 per cent of that needed to run the trains. (Normal earnings were nearer five shillings (£0.25) per train mile). The LNWR had already reached South Wales, under the very noses of Paddington. In 1862, as the Monmouthshire coalfield grew apace, the LNWR absorbed the Merthyr, Abergavenny & Tredegar Railway's magnificent mountain line up the Clyach Gorge to the valley heads. Within a few years the LNWR had extended westwards to tap millions of tons of rich steam coal from the valleys. Meanwhile the GWR, the natural bailiffs of this mineral rich region, slept.

The Midland board was as aware as Euston of the Welsh riches and cast its eyes to the western anthracite coalfield near Swansea. Taking a leaf from the LNWR's book, Derby befriended and then absorbed a series of poverty-stricken, over-extended cross-country lines just to the north of the coal valleys.

The first to succumb to the Derby overtures was the Hereford, Hay & Brecon. This rural line was built upon the track of the Hay Railway, a venerable tramway dating back to the early years of the 19th Century. Opened in 1817–18 with a 3ft 6in gauge, serving the gentle country between the end of the Brecon & Abergavenny canal and the Wye at Hereford, the old Hay Railway provided a pair of flanged tracks for horse-drawn trams. It ran calmly for nearly 50 years, until in 1862–64 it was converted to a standard gauge railway, the Hereford, Hay & Brecon. It was worked by the contractor, Savin, for a while until a Gilbertian comedy forced the line into the arms of the ever-ready Midland, while Paddington, again, slept. In July 1865 the HH&B had amalgamated with the equally impoverished Brecon & Merthyr Railway. Someone had overlooked the wishes of the B&M preference shareholders and the lines found themselves in Chancery, where the amalgamation was declared void. The unfortunate HH&B was forced into receivership on the technicality that the B&M had also failed to pay its debenture holders. The contractor Savin was also bankrupt, leaving the HH&B without an operator! Initially the B&M took over the trains, then thankfully disappeared from the scene. A brief period of working by the Mid-Wales was followed by overtures from Derby, which first operated and then absorbed the thankful HH&B in 1886.

The Midland next cast its covetous eyes towards the Swansea Vale Railway, an industrial line serving a series of metal manufactories along the River Towy at Swansea. Built by the smelter owners, the SVR was the only link for men as well as materials into these works. The Swansea valley had attracted a large number of copper and zinc smelters, whose fumes destroyed all vegetation along the narrow valley, making it one of the most polluted places on earth. Not a blade of grass grew within miles, and the life expectancy of the unfortunates who worked in the smelters was short. The Swansea valley attracted so much traffic that lines were built along both sides of the valley, joining at Glais and with the Neath & Brecon at Ynys-y-Geinon Junction. The SVR became too big an undertaking for the smelter owners to manage and in 1867 it fell into the arms of Derby. Thus did the Midland reach Swansea and the western coalfields. Passengers were neglected and the Swansea terminus at St Thomas was even less prepossessing than Victoria of the LNWR. Although the GWR had slept while the 'English' lines had gained entry to Wales, passengers from Swansea normally used the clean and well-sited GWR station at High Street. Derby never really took its Welsh extension seriously!

Direct to Sheffield—at Last

Although the first railway to Sheffield, the Sheffield & Rotherham was opened in 1840, the great steel city was left at the end of an inconveniently placed branch line, connecting with London trains at Masborough. By 1867 the town council was beyond its patience and wrote to the Chairman of the Midland Railway complaining about poor London connections. The S&R terminus at the Wicker was overcome by traffic and delays at Masborough were becoming intolerable. Samuel Beal, the Midland Chairman, replied promising a direct line up from Chesterfield, to be built within two years.

To the astonishment of the Midland board the Sheffield authorities did not shout for joy. Instead they backed an expensive speculation by the contractors Brassey and Field, called the Sheffield, Chesterfield, Bakewell, Ashbourne, Stafford and Uttoxeter Junction Railway! This unlikely line would tackle the Derbyshire Hills to join the LNWR near Stafford, at a wildly underestimated cost of £1 million. Fortunately this proposal foundered in Parliament when it was discovered that its financing was doubtful in the extreme. Instead Sheffield, in the MR, gained the sensible though expensive route through Dronfield and Totley to a station at Pond Street in Sheffield. One notable feature was the provision of electric lighting at all stations. The line connected with the MS&L at Nunnery Junction and with the old S&R at the appropriately named Grimesthorpe Junction.

Sheffield Midland station was completely renewed in 1905 as the present well loved InterCity station. Sheffield is well served by 'Midland' with its elegant cab porch, excellent information desk, pleasant refreshment rooms and easy access to trains. This station is now effectively the Northern terminus of the old Midland line to Leeds, which is more readily reached from King's Cross. Sheffield Midland is

Midland Stations – Sheffield (Midland): The fine *porte-cochère* still serves to protect Sheffield passengers from the Yorkshire weather – even in 1985. This station still has the leisurely air of the Midland about it, enhanced by a fine, brightly decorated buffet and a large warm travel centre. Oh that London trains could speed down the Erewash Valley to Leicester and St Pancras in under two hours instead of calling at Nottingham or Derby, adding half-an-hour to the journey! *Author.*

London Coal Drops: The London coal trade in Edwardian days was vast. Train after train would trundle south from Toton Yards to Cricklewood, whence coal was delivered to over 30 coal drops and yards around the Metropolis. These large drops near St Pancras were among the busiest, yielding coal to merchants who hawked it around the streets of London, for burning in the open grates of terraces and mansions in streets 'wide and narrow'. Note the horse-drawn traverser at the upper level. *National Railway Museum.*

still busy, with an hourly service to London, cross-country services to Manchester and Humberside, and the invaluable South-West to North-East services via Derby and Leeds.

In 1893 this line was enlarged to connect Sheffield to Manchester via the Hope Valley, whose Totley tunnel was the longest on the Midland. Hope Valley trains joined the Peaks route at Chinley, giving that bleak hamlet a junction station far beyond its needs. Following difficulties with the Woodhead Tunnels on the more direct cross-Pennine route through Pennistone, the Hope Valley is now the major line through the mountains to Manchester from Yorkshire.

The East Midlands Coal Lines

The Midland was lucky with its coalfields. Coal output in the East Midlands grew and grew through the second half of the 19th Century. From an extra 25,000 tons a year up to 1850, coal winnings expanded by a phenomenal 400,000 tons a year until the 1890s when growth reached no fewer than 700,000 tons a year. The Midland was well placed to benefit from this outpouring of coal, every ton of which was moved by rail. The expansion in the 1850s came as a life-saver to the beleaguered Midland, which with good timing went back to its origins and opened a highly profitable branch from Trent up the Erewash Valley in 1847. Originally only open as far as Codnor Park, this immensely useful branch was extended to Pinxton and then, in 1862 up to the NMR line near Chesterfield, making the Erewash Valley a through route.

By the end of the 19th Century the small coalfield along the Ere-wash had grown into one of the largest coal-producing regions in Britain. Villages sprang up near the newly-sunk pits—lines of small cottages never far from the sight of slagheaps and winding wheels. Never far, also, from the sound of small 4-4-0 tanks labouring up the banks of this hilly land north of Nottingham, pulling endless streams of waggons or rakes of workaday third class coaches along a complex tangle of competing lines. The Midland's hold on this field was challenged by vigorous thrusts by the BN and Great Central, so that three lines crossed and re-crossed several valleys, each with its own station serving the small villages where miners' families lived amid the grime and industrial haze. Before the car came, a bustling network of stopping trains served the region well—now transport is by car or grimy bus, as all but a few ex-Midland lines closed.

The history of the other lines in the Nottinghamshire coalfield is highly complex and very interesting. It properly starts with the oldest tramway in England at Wollaton, four miles north of the Trent, near Nottingham. Between 1500 and 1508 the squire, Sir Thomas Willoughby, opened a tramway to take coal down to the river, letting the road out to all who would pay his fees.

Other tramways followed in the 18th Century, mainly down to the Erewash Canal. The longest of these ran from Mansfield to Pinxton. Engineered by Outram, who founded the Butterley Iron & Coal Company of Codnor Park, and by the younger Jessop, it used edge rails instead of the more common L-shape plateway. This line left the Cromford Canal at Pinxton, rose to Kirkby, then falling gently to pits near Mansfield. Horses were used to pull loaded waggons up as far as Kirkby, gravity taking over for the trip down to the canal. The tramway was taken over by the Midland, using a Royal Commission Certificate. The track was upgraded to form the Erewash to Mansfield branch.

The Midland had built few coal branches to the north of Derby, contenting itself with the Little Eaton to Ripley and the Ilkeston Town branches, before the GN aggressively entered the fray with its line from Basford near Nottingham, intruding across the Leen and Erewash valleys to Eggington Junction on the North Staffordshire Railway. Opened in 1875/6, this cheeky invasion by the GN came when Parliament was becoming impatient of coal-fed monopolies. Even Derby was violated by the GN at the (now disused) Friargate station. The Midland responded with coal lines from Basford to Bennerley Junction and from Ambergate to Pye Bridge. Later came the Butterley to Langley Mill via Heanor branch, and the important extension from Radford (near Nottingham) to Trowell on the Erewash Valley, giving London to Sheffield trains a through run north of Nottingham after this opened in 1880. Most of these lines were to the west of the Erewash, but Mansfield was also served by a line up the Leen Valley opened in 1848 to the newly acquired Mansfield & Pinxton tramway at Kirkby.

Until the 1870s coal was difficult to win east of the Erewash because it was overlaid by limestone. Improved mining techniques then allowed collieries to be opened up in the Mansfield–Worksop area and railways followed to match their needs. The useful MR line to Worksop was built as the result of a threat from the MS&L to enter the 'concealed' field in the Mansfield area. When the MS&L proposed a branch from Retford, the Midland parleyed with the Sheffield company, which withdrew its Bill on condition that it had access to Mansfield. In return the Midland had a useful right of way through to

Retford, making a junction with the MS&L between Shireoaks and Worksop, giving a golden outlet to the north for the burgeoning coal traffic.

The Midland found itself almost inundated with mineral and goods traffic in the Nottingham and Derby area. Goods from the newly-opened routes to Manchester and Liverpool were pouring across the Peaks to swell the ever-growing coal trade. To cope, the Midland made two major changes near Nottingham, at Trent Junction and at Toton. The Erewash valley line had left the old MCR at Long Eaton Junction, giving access to Nottingham and Leicester traffic, but not for Derby trains. The early layout also included a level crossing over the direct Nottingham to Derby line. This undesirable situation was changed in 1862 with the building of Sheet Stores Curve, supplemented by a further curve serving the new Trent Junction station. Later in 1901 a high-level goods avoiding line was built for Leicester—Chesterfield trains. Trent, used for interchanges until 1968, was an isolated and windy place, loved only by rail enthusiasts.

In the 1870s the Midland opened up a series of large marshalling yards at Toton, just north of Trent Junction on the Erewash line. Robin Leleux's book in the *Regional History* series (David & Charles) well describes the growth of these important yards, now a focal point in British Rail's national freight network.

Today little remains of the North Midlands coal lines, and what is left is all Midland! Lovingly described by Howard Anderson in the *Forgotten Railways* series (David & Charles), the GN is remembered only by a long lattice bridge across the main line near Ilkeston. Only one of the three, (yes, three) lines crossing and re-crossing up the Erewash Valley remains; Ripley and Mansfield are served by passenger trains no more, only by the distant Alfreton & Mansfield Parkway station. Fortunately the Midland Railway Trust has preserved a stretch of the old Midland branch network at Ripley to remind us of a complex and once bustling passenger network.

6

SETTLE TO CARLISLE

Introduction

Only 16 years after the nadir of its fortunes, the Midland was so confident and mature that it was able in the early 1860s to cast covetous eyes at the expanding traffic to Scotland. The newly emerging upper middle classes, following Queen Victoria's example, had 'discovered' Scotland. Droves of Victorian families with their mountains of luggage, shoals of children, and numerous servants emigrated each summer to the Highlands. In all seasons legislators and churchmen travelled incessantly between London and Edinburgh, while merchants journeyed constantly to Glasgow, following trade in iron, coal and tobacco.

The public was spending a considerable £1,500,000 annually on travel along the LNWR West Coast route to Carlisle and the Caledonian to Glasgow; a further £500,000 was earned on the GN/NER East Coast route to Newcastle and on to Edinburgh by the North British. By 1866 the Midland rightly thought that it should be able to attract some of this trade away from the LNWR and the GN. Indeed, some trains ran from King's Cross to the 'Little North Western' via Leeds then via the Ingleton to Low Gill line to the old Lancaster & Carlisle. Schedules were reasonable on paper, but in the event journeys to Scotland via the Midland were fraught with delays due to the spoiling tactics of the LNWR which refused to co-operate with the Midland in any way. Connections at Tebay were non existent, and the Midland's Scotch trains were deliberately delayed.

In 1866 the Midland proposed its own route from Settle to Carlisle. A decade later, after many alarms, and an epic effort of engineering, it opened the gate to Scotland over the roof of England. At the other end of England, ever-increasing prosperity had opened-up the beaches of the South Coast to holidaymakers from the industrial towns served so well by the mature and expansionist Midland. In contrast to the Settle and Carlisle a through route to the Hampshire coast was opened up without effort with the close collaboration of the London & South Western Railway.

In the heartland, great changes were heralded by the discovery of large ironstone deposits in the Northamptonshire wolds. The Midland was not slow to exploit these, creating a new industrial base at Corby.

In these three areas, North, South and Midlands, the Midland expanded and consolidated its system into the third longest railway in the country. Easily the most widespread, it stretched from Poole to Carlisle, from Swansea in Wales across to a joint line stretching into the heart of Eastern England. We will tell of its men and trains later, but few stories of engineering endeavour can surpass those of the Settle to Carlisle.

Frustrations at Ingleton

Mr Allport was not amused! In theory the Midland Railway had a good route through to the border city of Carlisle and on to Glasgow via the Glasgow & South Western and by the North British Waverley Line to Edinburgh. The reality was different as Allport reported: 'I have been by a fast train from Derby to Ingleton, and then been attached to a train with six or eight coal trucks to be carried on to Carlisle.' The LNWR, which owned the vital connection between the former 'Little North Western' and Carlisle, stopped at nothing to prevent Midland traffic from reaching Scotland. Negotiations were started in earnest with the LNWR, but were blocked again and again by unreasonable demands. So in 1866 the Midland introduced a Bill in Parliament for a line from Settle on the old Leeds and Bradford extension, up the Ribble Valley, over the high moors and down the aptly-named Eden into Carlisle.

The LNWR attempted to deny access to the jointly-owned station at Carlisle Citadel but an anti-monopolistic House of Commons insisted on access for Midland trains to this most fascinating of pre-Grouping stations. Midland hopes were dashed as soon as the Bill was passed, by a possible amalgamation between the Midland's Scottish ally the 'Sou' West' and its former rival the Caledonian Railway, leaving the way to Glasgow barred by the close affinity between the 'Caley' and the LNWR. Allport counter-attacked with a proposal to join the Midland and the 'Sou' West' in an end-on amalgamation. Parliament, afraid of monopolies, thought otherwise and threw out

Settle & Carlisle – Hawes Junction: This busy junction on top of the moors was used for reversing the banking engines needed to help the heavy Scotch Expresses and Class A goods up the 'Long Drag' and up the climb from Carlisle. The turntable had to be protected from the Helm wind by a stockade of old sleepers. This junction was the scene of a ghastly accident in 1910 when the signalman at the end of a 12-hour night stint forgot to protect light engines returning to Carlisle from a Scotch express thundering through the dark. *L&GRP.*

Settle & Carlisle – Ribblehead Viaduct: This photograph, taken in mid summer, shows the area where most of the navvy shanty towns were built. The conditions in mid winter were beyond description! Few traces remain of the army of workers who built Ribblehead Viaduct and Blea Moor Tunnel, except graves at the nearby church of Chapel-le-Dale. Some shanty towns were named after battles in the Crimea, others after elegant areas of London. *Author.*

SEBASTOPOL

INKERMAN

BELGRAVIA

the amalgamation Bill. Back at 'square one' the frustrated Midland board was forced by a 'Manchester Party' among the shareholders to renew negotiations with the LNWR. Time had passed, and the Euston management was now more welcoming. All looked well so the Midland, seeing the way ahead to fully use its Ingleton route to the North, proposed a Bill to abandon the Settle & Carlisle line.

The L&YR and the NB now saw the extra traffic from the Settle & Carlisle falling into oblivion, so they brought down the Settle & Carlisle Abandonment Bill, leaving the Midland with an Act for a line that it no longer needed! To the eternal credit of the Midland board the Settle & Carlisle was built, and built well, costing over £3½ million. As a monument to human endeavour, it ranks second to none.

The Settle to Carlisle

Only a Wordsworth could describe the wild country through which the Midland thrust the Settle to Carlisle and only a Shakespeare could adequately describe its making. It can be compared in its mountain challenge to the Rhaetian Railway of Switzerland and to the strategic line built through the Khyber Pass, except that the Settle to Carlisle was a main express route. Not for the Midland the two 15mph trains a week of the Khyber or the electric comfort of the Rhaetian. Their Tasmanian engineer, Sharland, had plotted a route across the gale-swept moors on the top of England. The building of this last main line to be hewn out of the earth by pick and shovel is a saga in itself—once built, it was a fearsome railway to work as the forces in the hills fought against the thin metals invading the great wastes between the massive peaks of Ingleborough, Whernside, and the hulking mass of Pen-y-Ghent.

Generations of Midland fireman spat on their hands and squared their shoulders before settling to fire up the 'Long Drag', ten miles of punishing 1 in 100 from south of Settle station up the Ribble Valley to Blea Moor Tunnel, as the main Scotch expresses thundered up the Bray at timings set to compete with the flatter West Coast route of the LNWR through Tebay and over Shap. Sharland had plotted a ruling gradient of 1 in 100 for the 10 of the 15 miles up the infant Ribble to Blea Moor. His route passed just out of sight of Stainforth Force, then to the village of Horton-in-Ribblesdale, huddling under the great whale-like mass of Pen-y-Ghent, (named from a still-used language more like Welsh than English); the earth works near Horton were

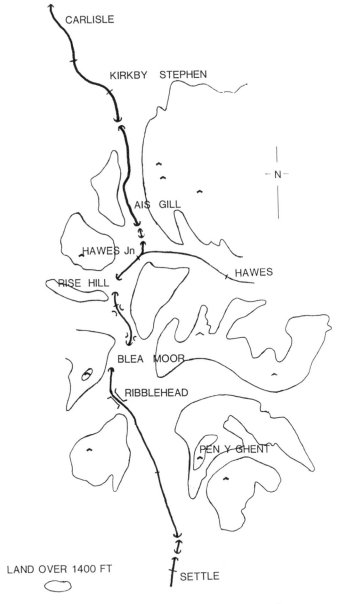

Map of the mountain section, Settle & Carlisle line

made a nightmare by the boulder clay, hard as granite when dry but a slurry when wet. Beyond Horton the line edged around the shoulder of Ingleborough, gaining height to emerge in the water-drenched saddle between Ingleborough and Whernside at a place called Batty's Wife's Green. At this spot on the top of England, soaked by 100 inches of rain a year, Sharland planned a series of great works, dominated by the Ribblehead Viaduct. Battered by 100 years of gales and snowstorms the viaduct now crumbles and its safety has put the future of the Settle to Carlisle in doubt. A mile to the north, the railway contractors built the greatest tunnel on the Midland system at Blea Moor, thrusting through an outcrop of Whernside into Dent Dale and Garsdale.

Sharland's line passed a summit within the tunnel, emerging across upper Dent Dale on a viaduct almost as grand as Batty Green. The surveyor then cut across the hills over the Arten Gill Viaduct and through Rise Hill Tunnel to Garsdale, where a small branch led off to the remote moorland town of Hawes. Hawes Junction, busy day and night with banking engines atop the open moors, was a fierce place on a winter's night; we will have to return sadly to tell of a tragedy caused by the bleak conditions. Buffeted by constant winds, the Hawes turntable was shielded by a fence of old sleepers after the dreaded Helm wind had caught a goods locomotive, spinning it round and round out of control. The line's summit is at Ais Gill Moor, 1167ft above sea level and 23 miles from Settle. Towards Carlisle the line descends at 1 in 100 for ten miles before reaching the beautiful Eden Valley and a slow gentle drop to the Citadel Station, passing Kirkby Stephen the first settlement of any size after Settle, where a branch of the North Eastern Railway passed under the Midland, looping round to meet the Settle & Carlisle again at the small town of Appleby.

The Shanty Towns

On Batty's Wife's Green lay the most challenging constructions and the most difficult conditions, so the contractors chose this spot to start their labours. Easier stretches of line would be started later and finished quicker.

Before the first turf was cut in 1870, the contractors gained access to the Blea Moor sites by building crude tramways across the moors from the Ingleton to Hawes road, clawing their way up the sides of the great hills with gradients of 1 in 16 around vicious curves. A massive windlass pulled three stationary engines up to the tunnel section on the very top of the mountain, to be set up to work day and night pulling materials up at the tunnel mouths and lowering bricks and other necessities to the seven working shafts. Sixteen gangs of eight men, each working by candle light, drove the 2629yd tunnel in four years, using the newly-invented dynamite to blast their way through the rocks.

The great viaduct at Batty Green, now called Ribblehead, was as big a work. Twenty-four arches stand over 100ft above the valley, an arch being finished each week while fine weather lasted. The first stone was laid on 12 October 1870 and the last in 1874.

The workers lived with their families near the sites of the great works. The largest encampments were near Ribblehead, on the side of wind-swept Blea Moor and scattered across the drenched mass of Batty Green, near that viaduct site.

The shanty sites were named after battles of the Crimean War, still alive in the folk memory of the navvies who were shipped out to help the army; others were named sarcastically for the new upper-class districts of London. Biblical names were used widely in most industrial towns in England for the worst slums—hence 'Jericho' and 'Jerusalem'.

In 1870 about 110 hutments were erected hastily between Ribblehead and the Denthead viaduct site, housing the many masons, carpenters, labourers, cement men, miners, mechanics and tunnel men, all with their women companions and children. The wooden huts had tiny compartments for family, for cooking and for lodgers! Two thousand people existed on Batty Green, with its perpetual rain

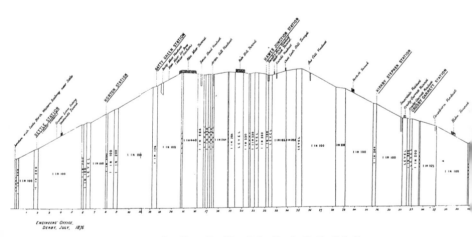

Gradient Profile of the Settle & Carlisle line

draining into the oozy bog. Even in mid-summer it is a desolate spot; to live there in winter is unimaginable. The page from the burial register of the small Chapel-le-Dale shows the terrible toll taken on children's lives by the appalling conditions. Pay was good by the standards of the 1870s, but it needed to be! Smallpox raged in 1871 and a smallpox hospital erected at Batty Green included an oven to 'bake' patients' clothes. For once, hygiene was met in the filthy pox infested camps.

The men used nicknames to hide identities—'Devon Sam' would co-habit with 'Leeds Polly', attracted to the 25 shillings (£1.25) a day earned by labourers. Masons, many from Wales, earned a princely daily 35 shillings (£1.75) but working conditions made them strike for more. The worst work was in Blea Moor Tunnel, where navvies worked 12-hour shifts, guided only by candlelight, hand-drilling holes for the new explosive, dynamite.

Social life gradually emerged at the camps—Sunday and day schools were set up, mission houses were built, shops abounded and contractors' bakeries made 2,000 loaves a day. The Midland Railway employed two scripture readers; contractors financed the school—43 pupils—at Batty Green.

Inevitably, alehouses mushroomed, followed by crime and fighting. Only six constables were stationed in the camps to keep the worst excesses under control. Navvies were cheated badly by landlords, one

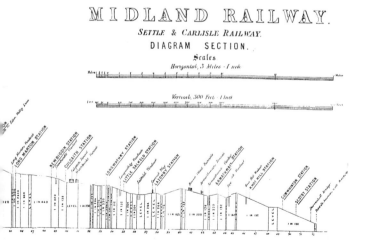

MIDLAND RAILWAY.

SETTLE & CARLISLE RAILWAY.

DIAGRAM SECTION.

Scales

Horizontal, 3 Miles · 1 inch

Vertical, 300 Feet · 1 Inch

Name.	Abode.	When buried.	Age.	By whom the Ceremony was performed.
BURIALS in the Parish of *Chapel le Dale or Ingleton Fells* in the County of *York* in the Year 18*71*				
William Dean No. 233.	Sebastopool	Jan. 22	11 month	Wm Harper
John Hollerenshaw No. 234.	Sebastopool	Jan 24	40 years	Wm Harper
Charles Bibby No. 235.	Sebastopool	Jan. 31	9 months	Wm Harper
Louisa Annie Thompson N. 236.	Jericho	Feb. 1	3 years	Wm Harper
Fredrick Little No. 237.	Inkerman	Feb. 5	4 years	Wm Harper
Tom Atkinson Little No. 238.	Inkerman	Feb. 9	1 year & six month	Wm Harper
Thomas Smith No. 239.	Jericho	Feb. 12	10 months	Wm Harper

Register of deaths from Chapel-en-le-Dale church

navvy seeking retribution by throwing his dynamite on the fire of the offending alehouse.

Industrial injuries were common; legs were crushed by waggons, arms by the collapse of cranes. Deaths were weekly occurrences, so that the churchyard at Chapel-le-Dale had to be extended, to become the only visible reminder of the huts at Batty Green—put up quickly and taken down faster. The great line of rails still stands, though, snaking through the lonely fells as a monument to the men who built it.

Working the Line

Opened for goods on 2 August 1875, extra works were needed before passengers were allowed nine months later. Stations were provided at Horton, Batty Green (later Ribblesdale), Hawes Junction (later Garsdale), Kirkby Stephen, Crosby Garrett, Ormside and Appleby in the mountain section. Ten more were built near villages in the Eden Valley. Water troughs were placed near Garsdale; using fell water, they were steam-heated in winter. With the opening of the line for passengers, five heavy Scotch corridor expresses thundered north each day, three of them in the early hours. Midland locomotives were small for the traffic, so double-heading was the norm, pilot engines detaching at Hawes Junction and returning light to Durranhill shed near Carlisle or to Hellifield, where a L&Y line fed Manchester. Local traffic was always light, and even in its heyday only four 'locals' used the line, contrasting with the great expresses and the stream of goods trains pulled by sturdy 0-6-0s.

A large staff of dedicated men lived near the line to work it. Working conditions were terrible, even in summer. The lonely signalmen had to climb up posts in the continual biting wind to charge lamps. Maintenance gangs worked out in the rain and the lazy wind of the moors—not a light wind, but one which goes through you! The locomotive crews, ill protected by the small Midland cabs, lived in Hellifield where the 'Lanky' joined the Midland south of Settle. The 'knocker-up' went his rounds in the chill small hours shouting 'relief for Leeds' or 'extra to Carlisle' outside the house of a driver or fireman.

Garsdale Head near Hawes Junction was a real railway community! The village hall was a converted room under the 80,000 gallon water tank of the junction station; it housed a lending library donated to the village by a wealthy regular on the Settle to Carlisle run. Isolated 'Salt

Lake' cottages near Ribblehead still stand, built to last to Doomsday as a monument to the men who built the line over the moors. The stationmaster at Ribblehead also ran a weather station, sending up balloons daily to record conditions and reading the rain gauge. Hawes Junction even had a bookstall and refreshment rooms in its heyday, unthinkable now when Settle has a staff of one. Before the Midland started refreshment cars, hampers could be bought for three shillings (£0.15) at Hawes Junction, to fortify passengers on the long haul to Scotland.

Before World War I, three day Scottish expresses ran on this line. Carriages starting from Bristol joined the trains at Leeds, Manchester coaches linked at Hellifield, after travelling over the L&YR. As a curiosity, the 'Lanky' insisted on its seconds, much less comfortable than the Midland's thirds, joining the Scotch trains. Semi-fast trains also carried Bradford portions, and some had Lancashire coaches.

Night trains were the 8.15pm St Pancras to Stranraer Harbour (for Belfast) and Glasgow, the 9.30pm sleeper for Glasgow, Dundee, Edinburgh, Perth and Inverness, and the midnight for Glasgow. Summer saw extras, especially after the 'glorious twelfth'.

The Settle & Carlisle was a fearsome line to operate; in Midland days both goods and the great night expresses passed in darkness, wind and rain hampering every simple outside task. Signalboxes were exposed to all the elements, one being placed at the very summit of the line at Ais Gill. Snow fell each winter, drifting when the Helm wind blew. The severe winter of 1947 was the worst recorded, with the line closed for nearly three weeks. Drifts filled more than one deep cutting; one trapped locomotive disappeared beneath the snow; even flamethrowers and jet engines could not clear the way. Eventually robust Class 4s of Midland design snowploughed their way through.

The Settle & Carlisle served the Midland well. Even in LMS and BR days it gave a fast run between the Midlands, Yorkshire and Scotland, but its vulnerability to severe winters had ruled it out as a competitor to the East and West Coast routes, and through trains stopped in 1980. This monument to Victorian competition and persistence, the last main line to be built 'by hand,' is probably doomed by the elements, which have weathered the great viaducts. Soon the trains may run no more and the moorland birds will reclaim their territory.

Completing the System—1

The Melton Line
In the early 1870s geologists had rediscovered the extensive ironstone deposits in Northamptonshire, known to the Romans. Suitable for the new Bessemer and open hearth steelmaking plants of Scotland and the north-east of England, they were easily won by opencast mining. Needless to say, the LNWR and the GN were active in promoting lines to tap so valuable a mineral traffic, so the Midland retaliated by laying down the 'Melton' line, opened in 1879. Built in two halves, with the old Hudson line from Syston to Peterborough in the middle, it left the main Midland line just north of Kettering. Running on well-built earthworks designed to avoid severe gradients, it met the Peterborough line at Melton and followed the old route, now upgraded by straightening Lord Harborough's curve to Market Harborough, then towards Nottingham, where entry was from the EAST along Hudson's other branch to Lincoln. So the Midland elegantly avoided the tiresome reversal for through trains in Nottingham, and with the same stroke tapped the great Northamptonshire iron fields. The Melton line became the main route to Nottingham, bringing it within $2\frac{1}{4}$ hours of St Pancras, better than the 1950s timings!

Corby Works
The Melton line gave life to a great industry in the middle of Northamptonshire, now also sadly diminished. Steelmaking in the 1920s was in a very sorry way, run down and depressed by years of neglect. The whole industry in Britain was at its knees, starved of new investment. In Scotland industry was very run down. Years of trade depression had left a scattered group of small works fighting to keep alive. A visionary Scot, Allan Macdiarmid, made a revolutionary proposal—to set up an entirely new plant, making steel and tubes on the same site right on top of the iron ore beds in Northamptonshire. The cost of moving ore to the works was more than moving the less bulky final product to the markets for tubes around Birmingham, not too far from the new plant site. The chosen site lay in the parish of Corby, near Kettering, and hard by the Melton line! Money was raised from the Bank of England and steel first was made in the massive works in 1934. Making 300,000 tons a year of tube quality steel in a Bessemer plant, the great works employed almost 10,000 men in its time. The tube making facilities were and still are the best in the world and the plant was manned by Scots from the old Monkland area—Corby still has a Scottish flavour. Technical developments

made coastal steelworks more profitable in later years, so the steel-making at Corby closed in the 1970s. It still has a large tube plant, making exceptionally high quality products. The Melton line was also surplus to requirements, and closed north of Corby in 1970. Corby no longer has a passenger service, but may re-open to serve a proposed leisure complex.

Completing the System—2

The Old Slow and Dirty

No greater contrast could be imagined than that between the Settle to Carlisle and the next addition to the Midland network. The Somerset & Dorset was the result of an amalgamation between two poverty-stricken rural lines in Wessex, the Somerset Central and the Dorset Central. From 1862 these lines joined to form a route across the West of England peninsula, hopefully to cut out the dangerous sea voyage around Land's End. In 1863 the route between Burnham on the Bristol Channel and Wimborne near Poole was completed, with the LSWR allowing trains from the S&D to reverse at Wimborne onto its line to Poole with its active harbour. Just as the S&D was getting its act together the Overend & Gurney scandal of 1866 dried up the money for railway development. Receivership followed, when loco-motives ran with plates announcing their true ownership by creditors.

The Midland in 1870 had opened a branch from its Bristol line as far as Bath. The S&D with the spirit of a true gambler's last throw, built a 'branch' from Evercreech to Bath, using a coal tramway for part of its route. Seven major viaducts and three tunnels were needed to drive the line through the Mendips. Gradients were severe, with 1 in 50 common. The new line opened in 1874 with high hopes of life-giving traffic from the Midlands to the Channel ports. With standard gauge to the South Coast at last, (avoiding transhipment to the broad), goods traffic expanded rapidly, to such an extent that the poor old S&D could not cope especially as it was too impoverished ever to double its tracks. Manned by ill-trained men and youths, disaster was always waiting; in 1876 a series of human errors led to a head-on collision at Radstock, mercifully only weeks after the lease of the S&D to the Midland and the LSWR.

The lease was not without scandal. The gentlemanly GWR had foolishly consulted the LSWR management, which over the weekend drew up a counter deal with the ever-ready Derby management. The Midland and the LSWR were accused of bad faith, but a perceptive Parliament allowed the take-over, a victory for the narrow gauge.

Soon the new owners took steps to bring order out of chaos. The track was put in charge of the South Western, with Derby supplying motive power. Gradually the new Joint Committee took charge. The reversal at Wimborne was abolished in 1885 by the opening of a new line from Corfe Mullen to Broadstone, allowing tains to run into the new Bournemouth West station. Holiday traffic soon came from the Midlands and North to the rapidly expanding new resort. Much-needed track doubling took place as well, and on the locomotive side Derby sent down some four-coupled tanks soon after the take-over, followed by powerful 4-4-0s. Derby also built 2-8-0 tender goods locomotives for the cruel 1 in 50 hills south of Bath. New through expresses from the North included a Manchester to Bournemouth express, later called The Pines Express.

The old S&D remained an individual line until Nationalisation, but it could not compete with the other cross-country lines. Even the 'Pines' was re-routed via Basingstoke in 1962. Closure came in stages in the 1960s.

7

LOCOMOTIVES AND CARRIAGES

Derby Style

The Midland locomotives were a quite distinct breed. Over the long second half of the 19th Century three Derby locomotive superintendents laid a distinctive hand on the course of British motive power development. The first, Matthew Kirtley, built sturdy express and goods locomotives, slowly improving designs to meet the increasing needs of the expanding Midland system. He built locomotives for the new Hitchin line, and for the St Pancras extension, with its two difficult banks near Bedford. Then he catered for the mountainous Peaks route to Manchester, followed by the challenge of the punishing Settle to Carlisle, built over the roof of England. All but the last of his designs were distinctly 'Kirtley' with double frames, many with outside springs above the running board, surmounted by large domes and Salter safety valves. Kirtley's early passenger locomotives were singles, but he was building 0-4-4s with two inside cylinders and Stephenson motion before the end of his reign at Derby. Goods trains were pulled by a vast fleet of rugged 0-6-0s, each design slowly evolving from earlier ones, as engineering materials and knowledge improved, leading eventually to the famous Class 4F of LMS days, arguably the most reliable goods locomotive ever built.

Kirtley was a cautious but effective innovator, who believed in line testing of new developments, never jumping straight into each new engineering 'gizmo'. However, he never let the technical grass grow under his feet, and the brick arch (allowing coal to replace expensive coke) was developed at Derby in Kirtley's day. Later when the Midland took a leading part in the introduction of automatic brakes in the 1870s, Kirtley organised the famous brake trials at Newark. He also lived through the Bessemer revolution, when steel became cheap enough to replace soft, weak, wrought iron. With typical care he introduced steel tyres and rails, using the wear resistance of the new

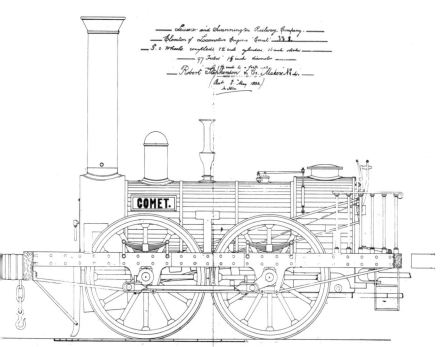

The *Comet*: An antique 0-4-0 built by Robert Stephenson & Co, *Comet* worked the Leicester & Swannington until replaced by Kirtley locomotives. It is commemorated in a nature park built on the site of the old L&S West Bridge Station. *Leicester Museums and Art Galleries.*

High Kirtley: Formerly No 156A, this representative of the 156 class was renumbered 1 in 1907. Built in 1866 at Derby with solid frames and inward-sloping weather boards, this class was extensively rebuilt, No. 156A having no fewer than four boilers before withdrawal in 1930 for preservation. Sadly it was scrapped in 1932. The Midland style of locomotive numbering on the tender side is well shown, as are the two styles of Midland carriage, arc roof and clerestory. *L&GRP*

material to advantage, avoiding the mistakes made by engineers who rushed to use the new steels despite the dangerous faults in the ingots made by the crude Bessemer shops of the 1860s. Only in carriage design was Kirtley lacking when he died in harness—the Midland carriage fleet was a collection of old four- and six-wheelers scattered over the huge system. On his death his job was split into two, separate locomotive and carriage departments being founded. The new Locomotive Superintendent, Samuel Johnson, was a grammar school educated engineer apprenticed to a Leeds locomotive builder, who rose to become the President of the Institution of Mechanical Engineers. He carried on the Kirtley tradition by meeting new motive power challenges with well tried, conservative designs, building locomotives well up to their jobs, and much liked by the drivers. Johnson's well-finished locomotives were beautifully proportioned masterpieces of the mechanical engineer's art, although under-powered for the heavy trains of the end of Johnson's reign. Looked after with loving care, it was said by an old Midland engineer that Derby was a 'Society for the Protection of Locomotives.' Johnson started his days at Derby as an exponent of four-coupled locomotives, changing to a 'singles' man in the 1880s. His famous 2-2-2 'Spinners' powered all but the heavy Scottish expresses, when the long drag north of Leeds called for his equally elegant 4-4-0s. Toward the end of his days, Johnson introduced compounding to Derby. (In a compound engine steam first enters a high-pressure cylinder and is exhausted into two low-pressure cylinders.) The 'Compounds' became a Derby trademark and Johnson's successor, Richard Deeley, although only in the Derby chair for a few years, raised compound design to a high art. The 'Derby Compounds', by-words for reliability and ease of driving, were able double-headed to handle even the heaviest of expresses over the mountainous Midland lines. The compound was refined steadily until the LMS version won the post-Grouping trials convincingly, lasting until outclassed by the mega-locomotives of the Stanier era.

Following Deeley as locomotive chief, Henry Fowler, was a 'Works' man rather than a locomotive designer. Knighted during World War I for organising munitions manufacture, Fowler had no real grasp of locomotive design, preferring to develop concepts from Samuel Johnson's day.

Between the beginnings of the new railway in 1844 with its motley collection of locomotives, to the elegant machines of the Midland's closing years, lies a fascinating tale of engineering development, a steady improvement in materials and design to meet the ever-increasing demands for power and speed. New locomotives were built for each demanding route opened by the expanding Midland: the 'Peaks' to Manchester, the Bedford to St Pancras and the gruelling Settle to Carlisle. New locomotives for the vast goods and mineral traffic daily moving along the nation's industrial arteries came out of Derby in vast numbers—sturdy, tough 0-6-0s and indestructible tank engines, usually 0-4-4s. What a great contrast there was between the first years of the Midland with a new locomotive superintendent desperately needing new engines, to the last stately years, by then one of the major engineering works in the world planned by a President of the 'Mechanicals'. Back we must go then, to the first years, following the growth of the Midland locomotive through successive generations of development and improvement.

Kirtley's Early Engines

In 1844 the new railway had only a collection of motley and mostly inadequate locomotives inherited from the old companies. Some were remarkable pullers—others, such as the Sheffield & Rotherham's were a joke. In 1844 the new locomotive superintendent had to assemble a fleet of locomotives able to power the new railway's services—fast!

Matthew Kirtley's first locomotives, bought from Stephenson's and from Sharp Stewart, were 2-2-2 designs with outside frames. With these and a number of Jenny Linds from E. B. Wilson of Leeds, the Midland was well served for its Rugby to Leeds expresses. Kirtley, who was scientific and ahead of his day in his approach to locomotive performance, ran trials between Derby and Masborough. Both locomotives, a Jenny and a Stephenson, performed very well, a load of 100 tons not holding them back on this fairly steeply-graded route.

On test, an average speed of 52mph (59mph maximum) for the Jenny was a good performance in the late 1840s, surpassing even the GWR Iron Dukes. In service the Jennys and Sharps ran very well on light loads, reaching nearly 60mph when needed—the Jennys had the advantage of a high boiler pressure of 120 lb/sq in, giving around 4900 lb pull at 65 per cent of maximum boiler pressure. The Jenny Linds were a particular success, lively yet reliable, capable of a fine turn of speed. Ahrons tells of one smart run in 1848 when the new and thrusting firm of W. H. Smith, then a small expanding newsagent, laid on a 'special' to rush copies of *The Times* carrying reports of the Budget speech to Glasgow. The Jenny averaged 56mph from Derby to Altcrofts Junction, a fine turn of speed for the 1840s.

High Kirtley: This one made it! Now preserved at the Midland Railway Trust, No 158 was built to the 156 design in 1866 and preserved at Derby Works in 1947. With only two new boilers it lasted in working condition for 81 years. *L&GRP*.

Later Kirtley: No 1076 of the 1070 class stands at South Lynn, showing all the features of Kirtley's later designs – outside straight frames, high dome with Salter safety valve, even a cab. The spotless condition of this locomotive was typical of the late 19th Century Midland. *L&GRP*.

Soon Kirtley had to design his own locomotives for the Midland. He rose to every challenge, the Hitchin line with its banks near Bedford, the mountainous Peak Line to Manchester and the enormous growth in goods traffic. Kirtley's trade-marks were double frames, outside overhung springs, and large domes with Salter spring safety valves. Cabs were minimal, comprising at best, an awning from the spectacle plate. His goods engines were always 0-6-0's, evolving slowly in design and growing vastly in numbers.

Kirtley's skill in locomotive design is best seen in the way he and his staff tackled the problem of coal burning. Early locomotives burned coke made expensively in coke ovens—relaxation of regulations about the use of smokeless fuel on railways suggested the replacement of coke by cheaper coal. Many weird and wonderful suggestions were tried to make coal-burning efficient—double fireboxes, air-inducing steam jets, enormous firegrates were the most sensible ideas tested. Charles Markam, the Derby outdoor locomotive superintendent solved the problem with the simple but effective brick arch, used in generations of later locomotives. Ahrons, describing Markam's success, attributes it to the Midland's use of locomotives with large free-steaming fireboxes for their trials. This gave the burning gases time for complete combustion before disappearing into the boiler tubes. The Nottinghamshire coal used on the Midland was not quite up to the best Welsh steam coal, needing 21 lb/mile compared to 19 lb/mile of Rhondda, but the high arch allowed any reasonable coal to be used instead of expensive coke.

The young Kirtley showed his practical approach to design by building Derby locomotives based squarely on the *Jenny Lind*, adapted slowly by realistic improvements in details. Between 1850 and 1855, Kirtley built many sturdy 2-2-2s based on the Jennys, quite a few ending their days much later as 0-6-0 goods locomotives.

Then in 1859 appeared the first of a series of 6ft 8in singles for express work with large 15in by 22in cylinders, raised firebar casings, separated from the boiler by a polished copper ring. These locomotives, the No 1 class, did sterling work in the early 1860s, when excursion traffic to London (King's Cross) was carried in long heavy rakes of six-wheelers overflowing with passengers. Although Kirtley had started using plate frames for his goods locomotives, these had sandwich frames, with short driving horns united by rectangular tie bars. Cabs as usual were absent, leaving the tough crews protected only by a mini-awning above the spectacle plate. This class showed how Kirtley set a pattern of fine attention to detail which still is a Derby trademark. He designed gunmetal valve rod guides for their

Kirtley's Main Express Classes

Class	Wheel arrangement	First built	Cylinders	Driving wheels	Other details
136	2-2-2	1856	15in×22in	–	Length 22ft 6in. Weight 28tons 9cwt.
No 1	2-2-2	1859	15in×22in	6ft 6in	Weight 28tons 10cwt.
80	2-4-0	1862	16½in×24in	6ft 2in	Weight 35tons 11cwt. For Hitchin line. Largest of the 50, 70, and 80 classes.
70	2-4-0	1862	16in×22in	6ft 2in	
50	2-4-0	1862	15in×22in	5ft 8in	
30	2-2-2	1863	16½in×22in	6ft 8in	Awning over footplate. These were Kirtley's last 2-2-2s, and were 'high Kirtley.'
156	2-4-0	1866	16½in×22in	6ft 2in	Weight 33tons 5cwt. Double solid plate frames. Springs above all wheels.
800	2-4-0	1870	17in×24in	6ft 8in	Weatherboard only. Double solid frames. Steel axles. Later rebuilt by Johnson.
890	2-4-0	1871			More modern design than the 800 class. Full cabs.

link motion, bolted onto the top slidebars. With each of the two slide rods though separate holes, long eccentric rods could be lengthened, giving this Kirtley version of the Stephenson motion an extra degree of 'controlability.'

The largest of the Kirtley singles saw the light of day in 1863. Later locomotives of this class were built with deep slotted plate frames, the lower parts forming the torsion member between axles. These beautiful machines were used on the London expresses from King's Cross until the opening of St Pancras. Many lasted well; two went on until 1905, having spent their declining years (in rebuilt form) on the old Midland Counties and on the Gloucester lines. No 33 of this class also had the distinction of being the last MR locomotive to be painted green after Johnson changed to 'Midland Red'.

By 1859 Kirtley had turned to the 2-4-0 wheel arrangement for heavy duty express locomotives. His early essays at this type were not too successful, until he designed the 80 class for the heavy King's Cross traffic of 1862–63. With 16½in by 22in cylinders, the 80s did well at this work. Two smaller designs, the 70s and 50s, were also as successful with lighter loads.

Building on his experience in his cautious, responsible way, Kirtley designed the superb 156 class of 2-4-0s in 1866 for use on the Peak line to Manchester and for the St Pancras to Bedford line, both sharply graded. With deep slotted frames, overhung springs, the 156s showed the real Kirtley touch. One batch (Nos 1 to 22) lasted to LMS days, all still going strong in 1923, with No 4 spotted doing pilot duties at Inverness as late as 1928! One of this class, given the duplicate number 158A, still proudly steams at the Midland Railway Trust, after preservation by a responsible Derby management in the 1930s.

Beyer Peacock of Gorton built a batch of similar locomotives, marked by Beyer touches—copper-topped chimneys and characteristic double plate frames. Ten more were made as tanks for the City Widened Lines, but were replaced by 0-4-4 bunker tanks.

Kirtley's Later Locomotives

Traffic had grown to such an extent by 1876 that Kirtley introduced a series of 2-4-0s of great strength and staying power. Suitable for the punishing gradients over the Peak route, the 800 class had double frames, steel axles, 6ft 8in driving wheels and large outside bearings. Forty-eight were built in all, thirty by Neilson, the rest at Derby. Deeley later rebuilt many for the Settle to Carlisle run, one covering the 48 punishing miles from Carlisle to Ais Gill in 59 minutes with the respectable load of 130 tons. All of this class were noted for their good steaming and could be thrashed over the steep Midland gradients without running short of breath.

The second batch of Kirtley's later locomotives, the 890s, had inside bearings and an altogether more modern appearance. First built in 1871, they were the first Midland locomotives to have cabs instead of the puny weather board of earlier days. A batch of 20 was built by Neilson, followed by a Derby batch of 36. A few of this class were fitted with central buffers to pull the all-Pullman Bradford Expresses introduced in 1874.

One of the 890s was fitted with the newly designed Westinghouse compressed-air brake, for the Newark brake trials of 1875. A series of accidents had persuaded Parliament to form a Commission on railway braking and the Midland under its progressive manager Allport put a length of level straight track near Newark at the Commission's disposal. Nine locomotives from six companies were fitted with a variety of braking systems, accelerated to as near 60mph as possible, and stopped. The 890 reached 56mph, and thanks to its excellent Westinghouse system pulled up in the shortest distance. The Midland jointly with the GSWR adopted it for the joint 'Scotch' express stock, but preferred the Smith's simple vacuum brake for normal passenger trains. The LNWR surprisingly persisted with the lethal Webb design chain brake, even after several crashes involving the poor braking system.

Johnson Takes Over

Kirtley died in service in 1873, leaving a legacy of good locomotives, but a poor set of varied, weird and wonderful carriages. The Derby board wisely split Kirtley's responsibilities, appointing Samuel Waite Johnson as Locomotive Superintendent and Thomas Clayton as Superintendent of the new Carriage & Wagon Department. The fascinating development of Midland carriages under Clayton follows, but first we must finish the locomotive story.

S. W. Johnson was an engineer of the new school; born in Leeds, he was put to learn the art of locomotive design at the famous Leeds foundry of E. B. Wilson, builders of the Jenny Lind class. After a period with the GN, he moved to the GER in charge of the Stratford shops, then he was recruited by the Midland. Different in every way from Kirtley, the self-taught intuitive engineer, he was as successful

A Foreigner at Derby: Johnson, who designed many beautiful locomotives, must have been shocked at the utilitarian appearance of this Baldwin 'yankee' 2-6-0. Faced in 1899 with an urgent need for more locomotives and a strike by British locomotive makers, the Midland brought in kits of parts from the USA, assembling them at Derby, before hurriedly pressing the locomotives into service. They had bar frames – reminding us of Bury designs. The front 'dome' housed the sanders, the rear one a whistle. These locomotives were liked by the crews, not least because of their large cabs! *L&GRP*.

'Spinners': This fine photograph of a 'Spinner' shows a single-headed train pulling out of Leicester. The short rake of clerestory coaches is typical of Edwardian Midland trains. The 'Spinners' could easily handle such short trains south of Nottingham, but further north 4-4-0s would be needed to pull even small loads unaided over the Peaks to Manchester, or up the old North Midland line to Leeds. *L&GRP*.

in meeting the Midland's ever-increasing demands for locomotive power. He designed what many regard as the most beautiful locomotives ever built, the 'Spinners'. Never one to jump into advanced experimental designs, he produced fine, workmanlike locomotives, well liked by their drivers, his professionalism rewarded by the Presidency of the Institution of Mechanical Engineers, for which he wrote a Presidential Address of wide learning and consuming interest. On taking office, Johnson was faced with serving the newly-opened Settle to Carlisle line. Rebuilds of the Kirtley 890s solved immediate problems, but his first design, the No 1 class of 2-4-0s were not a success. Their 6ft $2\frac{1}{2}$in driving wheels were too small to allow the locomotives to run well, while the steel crank axles broke after only 40,000 miles. Replacing the 'drivers' with 6ft 6in wheels solved the class's problems and indeed Ahrons summed them up thus in 1925; 'all have done excellent service with heavy trains at high speed in their day and many are still at work.'

For the Manchester services over the Peak line Johnson built the 1282 class, again based on the Kirtley 890, but with a larger boiler and a changed look in the splasher and dome areas. First built by Dübs in 1876, Nos 1282 to 1301 were used from Manchester, with a few at Kentish Town. A later batch was Westinghouse fitted and worked Scotch expresses from Carlisle to Skipton. A year later, in 1877 seven-footers appeared on the Midland with the 1347 class, again 2-4-0s, divided between Saltley for the Bristol expresses and Skipton for the 'long drag'. At the same time the first of many Johnson 4-4-0s were built by Kitson, by adding a bogie to the 1282 design. A bigger, new design of 4-4-0 followed in a few months, the 1327 class. Big for their day, with 7ft 0in driving wheels, 18in × 26in cylinders and large boilers, they weighed in at 42 tons. They worked the fast St Pancras to Leicester runs.

Before 1882, Johnson preferred the trusted 2-4-0 wheel arrangement, coming up with a 'winner' in 1879 in the 1400 class, for the Leeds expresses. Mainly built with 6ft 9in wheels and 18in × 26in cylinders, the 1400s lasted in faithful service well into the 20th Century.

The first of the main stream of Johnson 4-4-0s saw the light of day in 1882. The 1562 class was rather smaller than the earlier 1327 class, but powered a fleet of fast Nottingham runs on the 'John Noble Expresses', named after the general manager of the day, and later coped with 'long drag' duties—all with success. The 1667s, built in 1884 had 7ft 0in driving wheels and large cylinders, but were always hampered by small boilers. Reboilered in 1886/7, their reputations dogged them still. A decade later bigger 4-4-0s appeared in the successful 2183 class. These well boilered locomotives ran mainly on the tough Nottingham to Leeds route via Sheffield. One batch built in Derby in 1893 had the first locomotives on the Midland to have piston valves.

Before telling of the most famed Midland engines ever—the 'Spinners'—it would be wrong to forget the army of 0-4-4 tanks built by Johnson. They ran millions of miles on branch services, notably in the Mansfield–Nottingham area. Stabled at Mansfield, and Nottingham, they powered trains over some 182 miles of coalfield lines, covering 20 different 'diagrams' all within 20 miles of Nottingham. The heavy Birmingham 'roundabout' suburban services on the King's Norton lines and the Redditch trains were also pulled by these locomotives. Over 200 Johnson 0-4-4 tanks were built to Class 6 and 1252 designs, earlier versions without cabs! Some even acted as express passenger engines, especially on the Bradford to Leeds line and the Somerset & Dorset. The S&D used no others for 'fast' passenger work until Deeley's time.

Johnson also had to power innumerable goods trains, and for these he designed fleets of rugged 0-6-0s. Later locomotives for the express (Class A) goods were fitted with the new steam brake. Beautifully designed, they were described by Ahrons 'probably the best express goods engines in the country, and were the most beautifully fitted.' These locomotives trundled the faster goods trains between London and the Midland towns for years, carrying hats from Luton, woollens from Leicester and many thousand 'express goods' loads up and down the line.

The 'Spinners'

In the 1880s it was decreed that none of the singles left over from the Kirtley years were to be used—ever! The district locomotive superintendent at Leicester, not agreeing with this directive and sorely tempted, adjusted the sanding arrangement of a Kirtley 'single' left mothballed in his yard and pressed the locomotive into work. It did well with the new sander and he kept it going. Inevitably authority at Derby caught wind of the misdemeanour and the erring man was summoned to see high authority and explain himself! Johnson was so impressed by what he heard that he instituted a new 2-2-2 design incorporating a sander using compressed air from the Westinghouse brake system, newly fitted to Midland locomotives. So started the famous free-running 'Spinners'. With good sanding these elegant locomotives, when double-headed, pulled everything the Midland offered, even tackling the Ais Gill summit. Relations with the Westinghouse concern were not too good. The American company objected on the grounds of interference with braking. A steam sander was soon fitted, and Derby went on to build no fewer than 60 of these most beautiful of locomotives over the next 14 years.

Ahrons recalls seeing one of the first batch, No 25, at St Pancras in 1887. He was captivated by the elegance of Johnson's concept, by the great 7ft 4in driving wheels and the simplicity of design. These locomotives proved to be as good as their looks, for with 160 lb/sq in boiler pressure and 18in by 26in cylinders, they could cope with all the express trains on the flatter lines. Economical in coal, their final consumption between London and Nottingham was only 20 lb of Derbyshire coal a mile when pulling the normal Midland load of 110–120 tons. Speeds were always in the fifties, even with 170 ton trains. They were liked equally by the drivers and the world of railway management, winning a gold medal at the 1899 Paris Exhibition. One example, now preserved at the National Railway Museum, has been quoted as one of the most beautiful objects ever made by man.

The First Compounds

In the early years of the 20th Century the words 'Midland' and 'Compound' became as closely linked as 'bacon' and 'eggs.' Seeing the success of a class of compounds on the North Eastern Railway, Johnson cautiously introduced a batch of four compound engines. With engineering judgement worthy of a past President of the 'Mechanicals' he had designed a real winner. With one inside high-pressure cylinder (19in by 26in stroke) and two 21in diameter low-pressure cylinders outside the frames, operated by three sets of Stephenson motion, these locomotives were very flexible in operation. A reinforcing valve was put on the smokebox side to allow high-pressure steam to be admitted to all cylinders when starting, otherwise, steam was allowed only into the high pressure cylinder and then exhausted into the low-pressure cylinders before reaching the chimney. With 7ft 0in driving wheels in a 4-4-0 arrangement, and a 195 lb/sq in boiler, these few compounds were an immediate success. These were the first of many fine Midland Compounds built after Johnson's time by Deeley and Fowler, his successors, who took enthusiastically to the path set by Johnson. Later Compounds were to win trials against bigger locomotives from the LNWR and the LYR in post-Grouping years. They were masterpieces.

Johnson Elegance: No 2601 *Princess of Wales* won the Grand Prix at Paris Exhibition, 1900. This superb example of a 'Spinner' has been cited as one of the finest machines, in looks as well as mechanical performance, to be made by man. Built in 1899, it was withdrawn in 1921, when train loads had increased well beyond its capabilities. A similar locomotive now resides in the National Railway Museum. *L&GRP*.

Midland Compound: Built by Deeley in 1905, No 1004 was based on the Johnson compound design, but with Deeley patent regulator and auxiliary high-pressure pipe and valve supplying both sets of cylinders, so that the locomotives always started on 'simple' and changed to compound when under way. This design was the epitome of Midland compound design. *Real Photographs Co*.

One further curiosity of Johnson cannot pass unnoticed. In 1899 a general shortage of locomotives to power the growing Midland traffic coinciding with a strike at the hard-pressed British locomotive makers, caused the Midland to turn to the USA. In 1899 Johnson ordered a batch of 2-6-0 tanks from the Baldwin and from the Schenectady Works in America. Owing to shortage of space at Derby Works these were assembled in the open air before emerging to surprise a public used to the elegance of the Derby products.

The Midland changed livery under Johnson's rule at Derby, from the dark green used by Kirtley, first to a lighter green by 1876, and in 1883 to a dull red, giving way to the famous crimson lake better known as 'Midland Red.' Painting costs had dictated the change, but the publicity value was immense as the new livery was beautifully and lavishly applied. The main parts of the locomotives were put in red oxide, then sanded, followed by two further coats. On this were laid two coats of crimson lake, pitched out in black and given two coats of varnish. The smokebox was black.

Richard Mountford Deeley

At his retirement in 1904 Johnson had set the essential pattern of Midland locomotive management—small, beautifully engineered, well maintained locomotives used within a rigid system of double-headed heavier trains. Indeed one (ex Midland) cynic summed-up this approach during the discussion of a learned paper at the Institution of Locomotive Engineers, by alleging that the Midland ran a 'Society for the Prevention of Cruelty to Engines!'

Johnson's successor, Richard Deeley, was carefully chosen to continue this pattern. A pupil of Johnson, Deeley had worked his way rapidly up the Derby managerial ladder, excelling in the more scientific aspects of his work. Sadly, company politics were not to allow Deeley to fully develop the Midland locomotive fleet to fulfil the promise of the Johnson years; instead, an engineering tragedy of major proportions marred his brief period of office.

Deeley's first orders were for ten 2781 class 4-4-0 passenger locomotives to a Johnson design. Smaller tenders were now permitted as the Midland had water troughs at Loughborough, Oakley, Milton, and high on the moors at Hawes Junction. An early essay in design was a pair of railmotors for the Morecambe and Heysham line, ordered in 1904. Sturdy units, they could manage 50mph when needed. Deeley was also called upon when just into his office to enlarge the motive power of the old Belfast & Northern Counties Committee, acquired by the Midland in 1903 and renamed Midland Railway, Northern Counties Committee—NCC for short.

Deeley's first and only major design was a set of ten modified compounds, typified by the famous No 1000 outshopped in 1905. Their appearance, with a raised running plate and a large cab combined with the rear splasher, was to set the look of the Midland Compound for the remainder of its distinguished life. The changes to the mechanics of the range were profound. Whereas the Johnson compounds had a complex set of controls to move from simple to compound working and back, Deeley sensibly arranged the compounding to be worked from the regulator. A small opening allowed live steam into both high- and low-pressure cylinders. Opening-up further closed an auxiliary valve and started compound working, with live steam first entering only the high-pressure side. No superheating was thought of at this date—at least not at Derby. In all 30 engines of this design (or close to this design) were built and performed excellently on the Nottingham and Manchester expresses.

Deeley was a thoughtful and highly organised engineer, who introduced a simple, effective classification system for all Midland locomotives, to denote their power and capability. Each locomotive was in this scheme, which outlasted Grouping and Nationalisation, surviving to the end of steam. This applied at first only to goods locomotives which carried the classification number on the cabside. The classification was:

1. Kirtley 0-6-0s except those with boilers set to 160 lb/sq in and No. 430.
2. All other 0-6-0s except 2736 class.
3. 2736 class.

Later the passenger locomotives were brought in:

1. All 2-4-0s
   4-2-2s except 2601 class
   4-4-0s of 1312 and 1327 classes
2. 4-2-2 of 2601 class
   4-4-0s except 2606 and 2631 classes
3. 4-4-0s of 2606 class.
4. All other 4-4-0s

Subsequently, class numbers were extended by a P (passenger) or F (freight) suffix placed in a prominent position on the smokebox, used also by the LMS and BR in later years.

Deeley's rule at Derby was then cut short by a series of management changes redolent of a lurid television 'big business' series.

The 'Paget'

The calm of Derby was disturbed in 1905 by an extraordinary order placed by Cecil Paget, the Derby works manager under Deeley, for a revolutionary design of locomotive. This unusual state of affairs was a consequence of Paget's appointment, his large private income and his close relationship with the Midland Railway chairman—who was his father! Deeley's views when he learned of the amazing new design are not recorded, but can be imagined. This strange locomotive had two sets of cylinder blocks, each having opposed rotary valves. The massive boiler was developed from marine designs and was equally at variance with conventional locomotive engineering.

No doubt Deeley hoped that this strange design would stop on the drawing board. It should have, but to Deeley's amazement Paget was appointed to the new position of General Superintendent of the Midland in 1907. He was then able to push through his ideas, admittedly at his own cost. After great expense the experimental locomotive was built. It failed on its trials due to steam leakage, and was dropped. The real tragedy was the way in which all normal locomotive development was stopped at Derby while 'the Paget' was being designed. Deeley well realised how the small engine policy of the line led to needless double-heading and expense, and he produced several abortive schemes for locomotives as powerful as the magnificent new ones then being built by Churchward on the Great Western. Deeley's compound 4-6-0 would have rivalled the GWR's best locomotives for power, but was never built. Eventually, when Deeley was told at a directors' meeting of the decision to split his post into two, he resigned.

The Fowler Postscript

On Deeley's resignation Henry Fowler who had followed him up the ladder at Derby, was appointed as the first and last chief mechanical engineer of the Midland. A fresh-air enthusiast, Fowler toured the works on a bicycle, wearing a straw hat! During World War I, Fowler was appointed director of production at the Ministry of Munitions, and was knighted for his services in 1915. Basically a production man rather than a designer, he designed only two new locomotives for the Midland, two for the Irish arm of the company and one for the S&D. The Midland designs were much-needed 0-6-0s, bringing the total stock of tender 0-6-0s up to 1,495, almost half of the entire locomotive fleet. The most-useful Class 4Fs were built during this period. The massive 0-10-0 Lickey Banker, No 2290, was designed under Fowler and completed in 1919.

Even taking into account the intervention of the war, the Fowler years were a period of stagnation in locomotive development on the Midland. At a time when the 'small engine' policy of the Midland was showing signs of strain, Fowler took no notice of the far-reaching advances being made on the GWR by Churchward. Yet astonishingly the Fowler régime persisted even after Grouping—of which more later.

Derby Works

Most of the pre-Grouping companies set up works to repair and to build locomotives. Four of these, Swindon, Derby, Crewe and Doncaster were outstanding and were a veritable 'First Division' of locomotive and carriage works. Each ruled by an all-powerful locomotive superintendent or a chief mechanical engineer, these works represented all that was best in the art and science of engineering, each following widely differing traditions. Lacking any cross-fertilisation between works, each was complete in its own tradition of design and methods of workmanship. Between them they made immense contribution to the growth of engineering in Britain.

Under Churchward, Swindon reached the pinnacle of locomotive design expertise by the turn of the century. Derby made small, beautifully finished, reliable locomotives with well worked out details based on a scientific assessment of the performance of each item, be it main bearings, lubrication, or steam production. The Derby creations were well described as masterpieces.

Derby Works' growth to greatness stemmed from the vital decision of the Derby board (made in Kirtley's last years) to extend the works inherited from the old North Midland and scarcely expanded since 1844. The expansion was well under way when Johnson took office, so that great engineer was able to establish Derby as a centre of excellence in design and manufacture. Covering 20 acres of tightly-packed shops between the Spondon Curve and the Derby Canal, hard by the passenger station, the works took in basic materials—steel, copper, brass, wood, paint, and so on—and turned out magnificent locomotives designed in its own drawing office.

There were shops for each stage of locomotive manufacture—turning the great wheels on massive lathes, boiler making by riveting, the Low Moor iron plates, forging the massive steel shafts with gargantuan steam hammers, bending tubes, riveting copper fireboxes, and then assembling the locomotives in three erecting shops. Each shop had its own character: the calm of the great machine bays, the dark power of the rows of forges, lit only by the red heat of the steel ingots, where teams of men handled massive forgings under the hammer until the piece was perfectly formed, the rows of blacksmiths' forges like a vision of Hades, and the great erecting shops where gangs of men contracted with the company to make a finished 'Spinner' or an 0-6-0 goods locomotive.

Life in the Works

Lads joined the works at 13 or 14 years, apprenticed to a trade. A fitter, for example, would spend seven years learning his trade, making vital tools in his first few weeks. Then years of hard work followed for the men—a start for each day at 6.00am, called by the sound of the works steam whistle, breakfast, then a dinner break and at last, the final whistle at 4.00pm. Six times a day the whistle blew, governing his life day after day. Breakfast was in a messroom, palace-like compared with most industrial amenities in the late 19th Century. A visiting preacher brought in by Clayton undeterred by the clatter of cutlery, read to the men. Dinner, a midday meal, was prepared from food left with the cooks at breakfast time.

Wages were fair and related to the skills employed. Discipline was just, but hard on a trangressor, with no recourse to 'procedure,' but employment was secure and eased by privilege tickets on the railway, slowly agreed by a reluctant board. Injuries were not common within the works, and were mitigated by workmen's compensation, and by light work for those no longer able to do the harder jobs.

Grammar school lads entering as pupils went through a first-class practical training by some of Britain's finest engineers and started their careers in railway work. A pupil could expect to join the calm of the design office after a spell in the heat and noise of the shops, then back to junior management on the shop floor before many achieved high office. The Midland grew its own engineers—Johnson, Deeley and Fowler were all products of Derby's fine education and management development.

Labour relations were excellent, with Johnson and Clayton as paternalistic bosses, ruling their large empires with firm control. There had been a strike of guards in the 1860s but never in the works. Midland men preferred 'petitions' to the management, some of which were granted. One, calling for a stop to the humane practice of employing widows of former Derby workmen in the upholstery shop, was refused firmly by Clayton!

Carriages—Midland Excellence

By 1873 Allport, the Midland Manager, planning his Scottish service via the projected Settle & Carlisle line, saw with great clarity that he would not be able to compete with the shorter and well-established LNWR and GN routes to Scotland unless he could offer the new middle classes something extra in the way of comfort. Wanting at the same time to expand the Manchester and Liverpool traffic, he plotted to give the new moneyed travellers a positive inducement to 'go Midland' in luxury. Acting with great foresight, he did two things. First, he appointed on Kirtley's untimely death an excellent man to the new post of Carriage & Wagon Superintendent. Next, he abolished in 1875 the second class, promoting the seconds to firsts at the same fares as the old 'seconds.' The third class accommodation was upgraded to the same standard of comfort as the former 'seconds'. By two well-planned strokes Allport had created a legend—the Midland carriage benefiting the increasing number of wealthy travellers and the less affluent alike. The other companies led by the stingy LNWR cried 'foul' in shrill accord. The Midland was not moved and started a revolution in comfortable third class travel. The Midland carriage became a hallmark of not only the line itself, but of all that was great in the British Isles.

As Kirtley had no great reputation as a coach builder his successor James Clayton, fresh from Swindon, faced a monumental task. Fortunately, he inherited a set of well-laid plans for building a large new carriage and wagon works at Litchurch Lane, just over a mile from Derby station. The new plant grew quickly, and by 1878 was ready to deliver the first of a long and distinguished line of magnificently designed and built luxury carriages. In its maturity, with five tracks, it covered 14 acres out of the 40-acre site. As Brian Radford said:

'Everything about the new Works was planned on a large scale. Foundations took a year to dry out thoroughly and the quantities of brick, ironwork and timber needed were prodigious. The space between the sides of buildings was kept at 85 ft. leaving room for five lines of rails, and the space between buildings ends 70 ft. enabling the longest vehicles to be traversed between shops to any of the lines of rails which ran the length of the inside of each shop. The timber and saw mills measured 320 ft. × 200 ft; wagon shops 320 ft. × 200 ft. and the carriage painting and finishing shops 400 ft. × 300 ft., equipped with 17 lines of rails, each capable of accommodating ten of the old fashioned four wheeled carriages then widely in use. Parallel to this line of shops lay the three groups of workshops devoted to producing metal components, fittings and wheels. The iron and brass foundries were capable of producing 2,000 tons of castings per year and the general smithy had 92 smiths' hearths.'

The first carriages turned out at Litchurch Lane were 54ft long, revolutionising British coach practice with their pair of bogies, a far cry from the old four-wheelers of the 1850s. They bore the Clayton hallmark of wooden panelling with edges covered by elegant radiused beading. Three rows of panelling at the eaves, the window, and at the waist gave a characteristically solid appearance. Six-wheelers were built for shorter journeys in the Derbyshire coalfields and north from St Pancras, still to high standards of elegance and comfort. Many had a smooth 'arc' roof but express designs often had a clerestory roof, a Midland hallmark right up to Grouping. Midland trains had a neat uniform appearance, matched by lavish internal fittings in first class, solid comfort in the third class. They lasted so well that the author remembers travelling on the 'Pines' in the mid-1950s in a typical Midland clerestory, and very comfortable it was! Midland carriages were superbly finished. According to Radford, between 18 and 20 coats of paint and varnish were applied to each carriage, each coat being allowed a day to dry, the full painting process taking about three weeks including lining-out and varnishing. Many of the primary paint layers were carefully rubbed down and flatted by pumice stone to a state of absolute smoothness, accounting for the mirror-like finish on Midland coaching stock at that period. The colour of coaching stock in Midland days was the renowned 'crimson lake' a rich hue used from the earliest days for the first class carriages of the company, extended to the third class carriages from 1864 and from 1883. Clayton's genius was recognised at the 1889 Paris Exhibition when he won the *Grand*

Prix with bogie carriage No 916. It had three first class and three third class compartments with lavatory accommodation for each class. The first class compartment for ladies had brown plush, cased in walnut relieved by gold chasings and mouldings. The first class smoking compartment had crimson morocco décor, while the non-smokers enjoyed blue woollen cloth upholstery with sycamore casing, maple and walnut mouldings. The third class passengers were content with the standard plush.

In 1896 Clayton introduced a series of beautiful clerestory coaches, mainly 48-footers with eight-wheel bogies. A few corridor coaches followed with the emergence of the new powerful Deeley locomotives, and after 1903 many new long-distance coaches had corridors.

In 1902 Bain succeeded Clayton, and built many non-corridor coaches 48ft long and 8ft 6in wide, arc roofed and with a characteristically 'round cornered' beading pattern. He designed a luxurious royal saloon No 1910, built in 1912, which still survives. A 59-footer with two four-wheel bogies, it is divided into three main sections—a satinwood panelled boudoir, a Cuban mahogany saloon and an oak panelled smoker. A green Wilton carpet and tapestries were supplied to the highest standards by Waring & Gillow.

The Derby coaching tradition continued after World War I under the new chief, R. W. Reid, who introduced a strong and light trussed underframe design. Coaches built especially for the newly-acquired London, Tilbury & Southend line were a great success, the design persisting into LMS days, becoming the prototype for LMS suburban coaching stock. Reid, who rose to high office in the LMS, made sure that the high traditions of Litchurch Lane were carried into the post-Grouping era. The works still lead the way in carriage manufacture with the Mark III BR coach, Derby-built and exported all over the world.

Brakes

It is difficult to imagine how early trains were stopped! Before the 1860s locomotives were not fitted with brakes, so when a train approached a station, the driver called for brakes by whistle. The fireman and guards then wound down their puny hand brakes, the driver put the locomotive into reverse, and the train shuddered to a halt! In a crisis, nothing could stop the train within up to half a mile, depending on speed. So many preventable accidents occurred on busy lines that even Queen Victoria was moved to register her concern at the woefully poor braking systems used on all trains.

During the 1860s steam brakes were fitted to most of the larger new locomotives built by the Midland, but carriages had no stopping power at all. Automatic brakes, applied if couplings parted, were in the future, and despite the promptings of the Board of Trade, financial tightness kept progress at bay. Eventually in 1870 Kirtley carried out trials of a chain brake—a crude device never destined to work well—and rightly abandoned it.

Then came a major breakthrough. James Allport had visited the United States, looking at the best in American railway practice, returning with two discoveries. One of these, the Westinghouse air brake, revolutionised rail safety. Cautious tests were successful, so the first non-automatic air brake was fitted to a few express coaches, in 1876 starting with that other American discovery, the Pullman coach, of which more later.

By the mid-1870s public concern was such that a series of comparative tests were organised under the supervision of the Board of Trade using the level, straight Midland line near Newark. Nine locomotives took part from the major pre-Grouping British railways. The Midland train, fitted with the automatic Westinghouse was the star performer, stopping from 52mph in just over 19 seconds.

The members of the Royal Commission on Railway Accidents were well pleased with what they had seen! Slowly, the Westinghouse brake started to spread through the Midland. The 1302 and No 1 series of 2-4-0s were fitted with these brakes new from the shops in 1876, as were the rebuilt 800s and 890s. By 1877 nearly 200 newer coaches had been fitted, and many rakes of older carriages. Then a mystery arose! A dispute between the Board and Westinghouse slowed down further work on the air brake and the Midland switched to the Saunders Automatic brake instead, Clayton lending a hand with the all-important coupling design. This system, used today on BR, was so cost-effective that it was widely adopted across the Midland in 1879, making it a 'vacuum' line. By 1889 a massive total of eight million miles had been run by vacuum-fitted trains with only six failures, easily the best record of any of the many brake systems tried in the 1880s and 1890s.

Locomotive Sheds

Leeds (Holbeck) and London (Kentish town) were the top sheds where the most powerful and the newest locomotives were stabled. Belle Vue also had locomotives for the Manchester expresses and

Saltley, in Birmingham for the West of England runs, but pride of place went to Holbeck and Kentish Town. Even an important shed like Manningham in Bradford had only tank engines to take the heavy Bradford trains on from Leeds.

Big centres like London, Leeds or Sheffield each had two sheds, one for the passenger locomotives, the other for an army of goods engines, usually 0-6-0s. At Leeds, there was Stourton; the 'goods' shed in London was at Cricklewood, while Sheffield had the aptly-named Grimesthorpe for goods, complementing Millhouses for the 'Mahogany', the enginemen's name for express trains. The majority of Midland sheds survived into BR days, not closing until the 1960s. Before then, great places like Saltley and Holbeck had fleets of Jubilee and Class 5 4-6-0s (the 'Black Fives'), while the smallest sheds could boast only a few class 1Ps and a Class 5MT or two. Wellingborough was a great freight depot, housing the mighty Beyer-Garratt 2-6-6-2s in LMS days. Wellingborough shed thrived on the coal traffic to London, and could carry out major repairs only just short of Derby's capability.

Midland sheds were usually roundhouses rather than the straight through type favoured by some other lines. The larger sheds had up to three houses, each with a central turntable and roads radiating from it, as in the National Railway Museum main display hall. Small sheds were sometimes close to stations, as at Kettering, where the interested passenger waiting for his St Pancras express could view the preparation of locomotives for the Huntingdon branch or the other local lines. In the cities land near the stations was too expensive, so sheds were located in the inner industrial suburbs, convenient for crews, who usually lived in the nearby terraces. Kentish Town comprised three large round houses near to the local station, but being several miles from St Pancras needed considerable light engine working. The goods locomotive shed was hard by the extensive sidings even further out at Cricklewood. Nottingham's huge shed was also well out of town, near Mansfield Junction. Well planned and laid out, it had three sub-sheds, Peterborough (Spital), Mansfield, and Kirkby-in-Ashfield, although Toton was a main shed. Closer in, Derby shed was built at Spondon sidings, an area given over almost entirely to the railway. In Leeds, the passenger shed, Holbeck, lay towards Bradford while the goods shed, at Stourton was well to the south–east of the centre. Holbeck was the bigger, with twin roundhouses and had Stourton, Royston, Normanton, and Manningham as sub-sheds.

In Sheffield, Grimesthorpe was built in 1860 to replace the old inadequate Wicker shed used by the S&R, and expanded in 1870 after the opening of the Chesterfield line, in the poorest and dirtiest part of Sheffield, near the astonishingly named Brightside station. This freight engine shed, with a large allocation of 0-6-0s, mainly Class 4Fs in LMS days, stiffened-up with a number of Class 8Fs to cope with a vast heavy mineral and finished steel traffic, passed to the Eastern region of BR and was demolished in 1962. Its sister passenger shed at Millhouses on the Dore & Totley line was an eight-road straight house built in 1902. Always the daughter shed of Grimesthorpe, it had a good allocation of fast-running Derby 4-4-0s until the Jubilees appeared. The third Midland shed in the Sheffield area was at Canklow, well placed to service the considerable freight demands of industrial Rotherham, where more steel was made than in neighbouring Sheffield.

Birmingham (Saltley) lay not too far from New Street, in the Burton direction. It looked after sheds at Bourneville, Bromsgrove and in LMS days, Stratford-on-Avon. Saltley was a reserve shed for the Lickey banking engines.

Working in a shed was tough. Boys would start from school as cleaners, rising to passed cleaners, taking occasional firing turns, then to fireman and passed firemen with occasional driving duties. Some would graduate to the top links, others were stuck on the goods turns. Hours were very unsocial. A 'knocker-up' would walk around the small streets near the shed in the early hours to get drivers to work in time for the turn of the day. At the shed, enginemen would first read notices, checking for speed restrictions, availability of water and even weather forecasts when taking a train over the 'Long Drag'. Preparing the locomotive took around an hour, the fireman collecting tools, detonaters and flags, testing the water gauges and steam cocks, filling sandboxes before checking the fire lit by a 'lighter-upper' in the small hours. The driver checked everything and did a thorough 'oil-round'.

On the road, the driver concentrated on signals—in the old days stopping an unbraked engine was an art. The fireman would maintain steam and keep the invariably temperamental injector feeding water to the boiler when needed. Hours were long, conditions harsh, but locomotive crews were reasonably well paid and did their responsible jobs with cheerful dedication.

8

HIGH MIDLAND: A GREAT RAILWAY

The Mature Midland

Without doubt by 1870 the Midland was a first-class railway, well in the first division of British Lines, keeping company with the Great Western and the 'Premier Line.' Completed (bar a few cut-offs) by the Settle to Carlisle, the trunk routes north to south and the west to north connected the manufacturing districts of England with their markets. The main line to Scotland and the North of England divided at Derby, one route thrusting to Manchester and Liverpool, the other north to Leeds and up over the roof of England to Carlisle. After the completion of the Melton Line to Nottingham and doubling of the Belsize tunnel four tracks led from London as far north as Nottingham, allowing the vast slow goods traffic to trundle slowly while the expresses roared past.

The other main line connected Bristol to Birmingham and the northern manufacturing areas via Derby, pivot and headquarters of the Midland, linking all England's manufacturing districts save the North East, where the North Eastern Railway ruled alone. The Midland ran comfortable rakes of smooth running clerestory coaches pulled by pairs of elegant crimson red locomotives, and the slow-moving goods and coal trains headed by sturdy 0-6-0s. The traveller was enticed to the Midland by a fulfilled promise of comfort at reasonable speed and fair punctuality. The coal owners and the iron masters were persuaded to entrust their products to the Midland by reasonable rates, skilfully and locally set to entice trade away from the Great Northern, the 'Money Sunk and Lost', or the 'Premier Line'.

Expensive or perishable goods were speeded on their way by express goods. The customer could pick and choose which railway to use in these competitive days, so 'sharp's the word' was the keynote of the times. The whole tone of the line was set by the General Manager, James Allport who, with the Chairman, John Ellis, had built up a set of provincial coal lines into a great railway, competing with the 'Premier Line' for trade. Later general managers followed Allport's policy of aggressive expansion into the new century. Midland passenger traffic rose by one million a year until well into the late 19th Century, goods increasing by the phenomenal rate of ten per cent a year.

This chapter tells the story of the Midland in the years of its greatness, from the completion of the Settle & Carlisle, through the closing years of Queen Victoria's reign, into the new century, through the high Edwardian era to 1914, when the world changed. The story is one of never-ending growth, of the Scotch expresses, the Bradford Pullmans, regular expresses of crimson red coaches pulled by elegant 'Spinners' or the new compounds, of the never-ending stream of goods, coal and minerals pulled by 0-6-0s. It is also a story of major heart-rending accidents, few in number but tragic, and of a slow progress towards safety. The story starts with a look at travel in that England, through which it ran and in which it prospered.

Late Victorian Travel

London, the capital of the world; a map covered with the red tints of the British Empire; over half the world's goods made in the United Kingdom; great poverty and deprivation for some; wealth for a few, a growing middle class—such was late Victorian England, its growing numbers increasingly urban, dependent on food from the colonies, the first industrial country. How did its people travel? Who travelled, who did not, and what of the comfort, the pleasure, and the turmoil of the Victorian railway journey?

The rich, unencumbered by taxes, journeyed in great style, migrating in force, following the strict social calendar of the times. They always went surrounded by armies of servants and mountains of baggage, between the great country houses and London 'for the season,' back again to the country, or off to Scotland for the shooting, often hiring special trains. Stationmasters would be in defferential attendance at local stations, touching forelocks, at the departure of the 'big house'. Just before the 'Glorious Twelfth' there was a vast migration of the wealthy to the Highlands, made popular by Queen Victoria. Train after train, regulars and specials, ran up all three routes, East Coast, West Coast and the Midland to the Highlands. The revenue from the whole Scottish traffic was in excess of £1 million a year from the 1860s on.

132

The Midland did well out of this traffic, as many of England's greatest landed families lived near its main lines, several in the 'Dukeries' north of Nottingham and Derby. The Duke of Devonshire patronised the Midland frequently, using his special waiting room at Bakewell. Most of the country stations on the Peaks route were large enough for many times the local population, thanks to the nobility of their patrons.

The expanding army of the middle classes, professionals, businessmen, bank managers and the like, travelled less grandly. Anyone then earning more than £200 a year could expect to travel first class on the annual holiday at the seaside, with the family and the two or more live-in servants, while *paterfamilias* would go occasionally to London or to a large city for business.

The author of *Our Railways* written in the 1890s, paints the picture well:

Many of the delights of holiday, it has been said, are far keener than those of daily life; but the tribulations are greater too. Undoubtedly this plaintive sentiment is the outcome of engineering a large family to the seaside. There is, to some sensitive minds, no greater ordeal, no more prostrating tribulation, especially if you have to leave your belongings stranded in the station at the journey's end while you desperately and wearily search for lodgings. Most convivial people are familiar with the humorous song *John Brown's Luggage*, and the gigantic task involved in handling it—the barrow piled high with boxes, hampers, bags, shawls, sticks, and umbrellas; the rush through the crowd on the platform; the search for a compartment; the work of settling down in it; the stern duty of seeing the luggage placed in the van, and the secret fear that the vehicle may be shunted and coupled to a part of the train that proposes to diverge miles away from your destination. All these things tend to upset a man's nervous system. He gets hot, anxious, worried; and as he takes a last scamper down the platform to see if the luggage is safe, and scrambles into the overcrowded compartment just as the guard waves his green flag and the train is on the move, he is every bit as flustered as the old lady who, on entering the railway carriage, counted and recounted her parcels in great agitation, and exclaimed in despair, 'Lor', I've forgotten the baby!' He vows that he will never take such a fool's journey any more—that the quietude and comfort of home are preferable to this wild stampede to a strange place. But next summer "the children want a change", and he goes through the torture again.'

Ordinary mortals could not afford holidays away from home. The average wage of manual workers who made up the vast majority of the population, ranged from forty shillings (£2.00) a week for the most highly skilled (which included engine drivers) to around fifteen shillings (£0.75) a week for the labourers and general minders at the bottom of the working scale, railway porters averaging around twenty-five shillings (£1.25) a week. Third class train fares were a penny a mile or thereabouts, so a whole family could not go far on those wages. Indeed the average cost of a single rail journey in the 1890s was around eighteen pence (£0.07) corresponding to a round trip of just over 30 miles. In any event for the working classes, holidays were out of the question—no work, no pay. The author's mother counted herself lucky to have an annual trip away, made possible by the generosity of the GWR to her signalman father. None of their school-friends ever went out of their small Welsh home town until entering 'service' at 12 or 13 years of age.

Travel for the Masses

Despite the economic pressures, a vast number of journeys were nevertheless made—a million extra a year on the Midland alone. Journeys were made to work using the invaluable workmen's tickets, available in the early morning before the higher orders wanted to travel. Such fares were often lower than the 'Parliamentary' penny-a-mile. Relatives were visited in neighbouring towns, visits were made to market for selling or shopping. Young men started to court girls in the next town or village; the author's father was expected to travel up the Swansea Valley Midland branch each Sunday for high tea at his future wife's home, too far from Swansea for even the most ardent swain to walk!

For all this to-ing and fro-ing, the most common reason for travel in Queen Victoria's era was the excursion. Thomas Cook started his world-wide business after a successful temperance excursion on the old Midland Counties Railway, taking thousands to a rally at Loughborough. The temperance movement organised many such excursions on each of the main railways, with the Midland laying-on a regular Sunday outing for the National Sunday League, leaving St Pancras at 11.35 am each Sunday for Derby, Matlock and Buxton. They hoped this would keep men out of the public houses, introducing them instead to the delights of the Peaks. Each summer thousands of Sunday schools hired whole trains for Saturday outings.

Without excursions, most people would never have set foot in a train; some Midland outings even included dining facilities but 'packed lunches' would have been the more common means of refreshment. Fares, at a halfpenny or three farthings a mile, were very attractive—under £0.005 per mile in modern terms.

The Midland had extensive excursion facilities by ordinary express trains, backed by special excursion traffic. For example, the cheap third class restaurant car corridor express which left St Pancras at 11.38am on Saturdays during the season was a first-rate express train. It stopped at Nottingham (in 137 minutes), and reached Carlisle at 6.38pm and Edinburgh at 9.35pm. There was also a 'Guaranteed' express excursion leaving St Pancras at 8.30pm on certain dates, booked to Carlisle at an average of 49mph, the train being continued by the Glasgow & South Western Railway to Glasgow and beyond. The Midland also ran various excursions between Sheffield and St Pancras (average 46.6mph), Manchester and St Pancras (average 47mph), St Pancras and Leicester (average 48mph), St Pancras and Bromford Bridge (average 43.7mph) and Bristol and Birmingham (average 41mph). On Friday nights a Scotch express excursion left St Pancras at 10.00pm, reaching Glasgow at 8.00am and Edinburgh at 8.10am. But undoubtedly the greatest social change came in 1875 when the Midland abolished the second class, upgraded third class coaches with upholstered seats and admitted third class travellers to all trains. All this was in keeping with the Midland's aggressive marketing policy—designed to keep traffic from its rivals at Euston and King's Cross.

These millions of passengers and avalanches of goods made the Midland grow. Let us now look at this aggressively expanding Midland Railway of Queen Victoria's last decades, how it matured into a major material railway, how it prospered on good comfortable passenger services, express and local, and on transport of coal, minerals and merchandise of every description in England's industrial heartland.

The Midland Prospers

The late 1870s saw a revolution in the Midland's financial strength; the benefit of the increased freight traffic to and from Scotland coupled with the new fast comfortable expresses to the North and the Midlands Counties had done wonders for the coffers. In 1876 a dividend of just over five per cent was all that could be paid out of the £1,064,205 available to the shareholders; by 1880 this had increased to

£1,406,440, at a dividend of 6¹/₈ per cent. In his last years as General Manager, Allport had the satisfaction of seeing his railway climb out of the middle ranks of railway shares to achieve respectability. The 'Inner Cabinet' of Chairman Edward Ellis (son of John), Allport, Clayton and Johnson, had by careful long term planning and determined endeavour made the Midland into one of the foremost railways in the land.

In 1880 a new team with John Noble as General Manager took over the baton from the old guard. They started the 'Noble Expresses', commenced an extensive network of through coaches, and established the Manchester services on a proper footing with the adoption of Manchester Central station as the northern terminus for those expresses.

Midland Timetables

In its maturity after around 1880 the Midland timetable listed main line services from London to Scotland, the Midlands and Lancashire, others from the West Country to the North and the Midlands, interleaved by local services. By the 1900 edition, the main section was over 180 pages in length with a 50-page appendix for special tourist services. One special section outlined the dining and sleeper facilities, another the excellence of the passenger accommodation. The main section listed the 413 through carriages run with other lines, with Birmingham to Norwich one of the shorter through journeys possible in 1900, Aberdeen to Southampton one of the longer. A passenger entraining at Gloucester, for example, could reach twelve other towns without changing, including far away Aberdeen, Bournemouth, Harrogate, Leeds or Newcastle. Best served was Birmingham, which had 23 towns served by through coaches, ranging from Brecon and Kingswear to York and Manchester.

The Midland main line services from London to Bedford look very much as today, with up trains going through to Moorgate on the City Widened Lines, but one lost route has been St Pancras to Tottenham and Tilbury via the London, Tilbury & Southend, with trains at two-hourly intervals. Many trains ran to Victoria from Kentish Town, where many long-distance trains stopped for the benefit of passengers travelling south of the Thames. These trains looped round via the City Widened Lines, under Snow Hill, across the Thames to Borough Road and then to Loughborough Junction and the Chatham lines into Victoria.

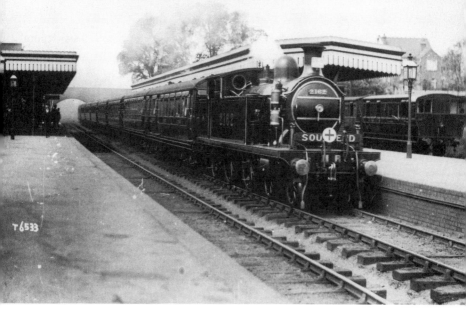

Lost Suburban Services: This photograph shows ex LTS 4-4-2T No 2162, formerly No 55 *Wellington Road*, on an Ealing to Southend service. This service ran from Ealing Broadway, through Mark Lane (now Tower Hill) to Barking and on to Southend. *Real Photographs Co.*

Double-headed: Two Deeley 4-4-0s pull out of Carlisle Citadel on a Glasgow St Enoch to St Pancras express. Double-heading was often needed for heavy trains on the long climb to Ais Gill summit and strict rules governed the maximum load for single engine working. The massive end wall at Citadel can be clearly seen behind the mixed bag of coaches. *L&GRP.*

A few services in the Midlands also have not survived, notably the Kettering to Cambridge 'flyer' which stopped virtually everywhere (even minute Twywell) the Midland timetable bravely noting connections from Edinburgh and Manchester to Cambridge, although who would go via Kettering to the Fens from Scotland or Lancashire is not recorded. Other casualties of time have been the Bedford—Northampton branch and the little line to Higham Ferrers, while Hemel Hempstead and Olney are no longer reached from St Pancras. The Leicester to Birmingham line survives, with fewer stations, but Leicester to Burton has passed away with the Melton Line. Casualties are fewer north of Leeds, being confined to the branches to Grassington and the Worth Valley. Let us hope that the Settle & Carlisle will not also pass into memories. Much of the 1900 timetable remains; granted, the Scotch expresses have been given to the old rivals either side of the country. Only a third of the Midland stations listed in 1910 have disappeared from the BR timetable of the 1980s.

The Scotch Services

Though in its heyday pride of place on the Midland went to the Scotch expresses, from the first days of the Settle & Carlisle, innumerable goods trains trundled between the manufacturing districts of England and Glasgow and the Clyde—iron from the Monklands, tobacco from the port of Glasgow, engineering products from the Clyde. Up to Scotland went goods of English manufacture, clothes, luxuries, and foods. In all weathers, mostly in the night watches, million of miles were logged over the 'Long Drag' by stout Midland 0-6-0s, pulling long rakes of loose-coupled 10-ton freight waggons.

Freight made the S&C profitable to the Midland, but the crack Scotch express trains made its name. Derby, with competition from Euston and King's Cross, had a secret weapon—the Pullman car. Allport had travelled to the United States to survey the latest transAtlantic railway practice, returning with two 'finds'—Pullman of luxurious carriage fame, and Westinghouse, inventor of the air-operated brake. The Pullmans, developed for the long journeys of the USA, were streets ahead of British carriages in comfort with their heavy bogie springing and lavish interiors. Even more attractive to the Midland board were the financial terms where Pullman stood all the financial risk, making his money on the extra charges made for travelling in the Pullmans.

The Pullmans were of two varieties, sleepers and day parlours, the latter being owned by the Midland, at a cost of £3,000 each. The vehicles, assembled at Derby from kits made in Detroit, were over 58ft long, large by British standards. The interiors, in a departure from British practice, were open with a gangway along the centre of the cars, like the modern InterCity 125 sets. The day coaches, known as Drawing Room Cars, had lavish swivelling arm chairs. The first, named *Midland*, *Excelsior*, and *Enterprise*, gave a superb service, with staff recruited from private service.

On 1 June 1874 the first regular passenger service to include Pullman cars went into operation between Bradford and London, the southbound train departing at 8.30am and reaching St Pancras at 2.05pm. The down train departed from St Pancras at midnight with arrival at Bradford at 5.30am. Lucky passengers were allowed to sleep on until a more civilised hour before detraining. In true Midland style this train made history by being the first British one which was both heated and which allowed passengers to move from one end to another, even though they had to negotiate the American-style open ends.

Unfortunately the Pullmans were ahead of their time and the original cars were later separated and allocated to express services to all the main Midland destinations. Later in the mid-1880s ordinary Midland carriages had so improved under Clayton's guidance that the Pullmans were used less and less, moving to other companies. They had made an indelible impression on the early Scotch and other crack trains of the time.

Coming back to the Scotch services, the early expresses from 1876 had portions on each down train for Glasgow and for Edinburgh, both with Pullmans. The morning 'down' left St Pancras at 10.30am, stopping at Bedford, Leicester, Trent and Sheffield, before reaching Normanton, where there was a 30-minute 'amenity' break. The Sheffield stop allowed coaches from Bristol to be attached, taken from the 9.00am ex-Bristol. By-passing Leeds, the heavy train was pulled over the 'Long Drag' by locomotives of the No 1 class, then emerging from Derby. A stop at Skipton also allowed passengers from the L&YR, Leeds and Bradford to join the train. All stops except at Normanton were short, and all locomotive changes were exceptionally quick. The two portions divided at Carlisle Citadel, before being entrusted to the Glasgow & South Western for Glasgow and the North British for Edinburgh. Overall average speeds in the region of 45mph were good for the 1870s, despite the heavy loads and hilly terrain.

The evening down train departing at 9.15pm was just as quick, but had Pullman sleepers instead of the drawing room cars. The 9.15pm made a brief stop at Kentish Town to pick up passengers from south of the Thames. From north of Sheffield it ran direct to Leeds, Wellington, with only a 15-minute stop for refreshments. Beyond Leeds the timings were similar to the day train.

After 1876 the Scotch expresses were speeded up in response to competition from the East and West Coast routes. By 1879 the 10.30am train reached Carlisle at 6.03pm, 22 minutes earlier than the 1876 timing. The arrival time at the 'Sou West' terminus of St Enoch, Glasgow, was brought back to 9.02pm from the 1876 timing of 9.20pm. Much of the time saved was due to the diversion up the old North Midland Railway route by-passing Sheffield, avoiding Bradway Summit and the Sheffield stop. The Midland board also intensified its attacks on the competition by making its trains even more comfortable. New joint stock, built to Clayton's design were deployed. Ten 54ft long composites, twenty 40ft coaches and ten passenger brake vans took to the rails, offering a degree of comfort not seen elsewhere in Britain. A tourist express left St Pancras each night at 9.15pm reaching Perth, thanks to the friendly North British, ten minutes ahead of the rival matching King's Cross departure.

The Noble Expresses

In 1880 after long and faithful service to the Midland James Allport retired from his job. Allport's successor, John Noble, kept up the Midland's aggressive attacks on its rivals with a series of smartly-timed expresses to the North. Using the newly-opened Melton Line, Leeds was reached in $4\frac{1}{2}$ hours, Sheffield in 3 hours 40 minutes, pulled by Johnson's 1400 series 2-4-0s, well able to cope with the heavy rakes of new eight-wheel bogie coaches turned out by Derby to even higher standards of comfort and smooth riding.

In the up direction times were also smart, just over five hours to London from Bradford, and 2 hours 40 minutes from Nottingham—no wonder they were called the 'Noble Expresses.' The fastest was the 10.00am ex Leeds which covered the 204 miles from Leeds, Wellington, to St Pancras at an average speed of 48mph; running speeds well over 50mph were needed between Kettering and London.

By 1883 Manchester was also well served, with a service better and faster than Euston's. Times for the up 3.45pm departure were:

Miles	Stations	Times,	pm	Speeds, mph
	Manchester (Central)	dep	3.45	
				40.00
31¼	Miller's Dale	arr	4.32	
	Miller's Dale	dep	4.35	
				45.75
62½	Derby	arr	5.16	
	Derby	dep	5.21	
				46.00
92	Leicester	arr	5.59	
	Leicester	dep	6.04	
				48.00
141½	Bedford	arr	7.06	
	Bedford	dep	7.10	
				45.00
161	Luton	arr	7.36	
	Luton	dep	7.37	
				47.50
189½	Kentish Town	arr	8.13	
	Kentish Town	dep	8.16	
191¼	St Pancras	arr	8.20	

On the West of England main line typical timings were in 1883:

Stations	Times,	pm	Speeds, mph
Derby	dep	12.35	
			51.75
Birmingham	arr	1.24	
Birmingham	dep	1.30	
			46.00
Cheltenham	arr	2.29	
Cheltenham	dep	2.33	
			35.50
Gloucester	arr	2.44	
Gloucester	dep	2.48	
			45.30
Bristol	arr	3.37	

By the end of the century, despite better speeds on the Euston Line, Manchester expresses were a bit smarter, the 9.00am in 1900 running as follows:

Stations	Times,	am/pm	Speeds, mph
St Pancras	dep	9.00	52.90
Kettering	arr	10.22	52.60
Kettering	dep	10.26	
Nottingham	arr	11.25	44.10
Nottingham	dep	11.30	
Marple	arr	12.51	40.00
Marple	dep	12.54	
Manchester	arr	1.15	

Midland expresses were still kept to speeds of around 50mph. Ahrons quotes the long-established 2.10pm Scotch express timings as follows in 1893:

Stations	Times,	pm	Speeds, mph
St Pancras	dep	2.10	
			51.90
Kettering	pass	3.34	
Nottingham	arr	4.33	
Nottingham	dep	4.37	
			40.50
Sheffield	arr	5.37	
Sheffield	dep	5.41	
			49.40
Leeds	arr	6.29	
Leeds	dep	6.34	
			48.75
Hellifield	arr	7.19	
Hellifield	dep	7.22	
(Ais Gill Box)	(pass	8.00)	49.20
Carlisle	arr	8.55	

These times are lethargic by today's standards, but still acceptable in the 1890s. Soon, change was at hand.

Enter Sir Guy

No one can claim that the 1890s were a time of great enterprise on the Midland. After the period of expansion, led by James Allport and John Noble, the line rested on its laurels under George Turner. The 'Race to the North' by the rival lines to Scotland passed by the Midland's managers as if beneath their notice. It is hard to imagine Allport not responding to that challenge in some way, but Turner allowed the 'Races' publicity to go to the rivals at Euston and King's Cross. Nevertheless, the line was prosperous, and Turner's policy of 'freight first' was paying the shareholders well.

The Derby board of the 1890s believed in maximum traffic at minimum expense. Dividends were always in the region of seven per cent, well up the table of British railway dividends. However, the vast coal traffic was taking its toll by the shocking unpunctuality of passenger services—even the crack expresses were slowed by crawling coal trains, and the Midland became a byword for lateness. By 1901 a member of the board, Lord Farrar, took matters in hand and reorganised the express timetable with the Scotch services taking priority. By 1910 the Midland had so improved that nine stately expresses left St Pancras daily for Scotland. The fastest was the 11.50am, non-stop to Carlisle (with locomotive change at Shipley). Most trains stopped at Leicester, many at Trent, one only at Nottingham, where it reversed, making Nottingham a surprising backwater.

Lancashire services benefited as well with several fast trains a day. Three ran to Manchester central in under four hours, using the new Disley Tunnel and the Stockport 'by-pass'. The 10.00am was particularly smart, going via Manchester Victoria on to Blackburn. There was no provision for an evening train—a long-lasting feature of Manchester services, which took over three hours even in the 1950s, with the last sensible train leaving at 6.00pm. Now an up Evening Pullman leaves as late as 20.20 taking only 2 hours 40 minutes to reach Manchester Piccadilly. Lord Farrar also smartened-up the important West of England trains to match GWR competition, as part of the Midland revival.

By 1904 the system was saturated, the victim of its own success.

Only the passenger and Class A express goods trains ran to timetable. No one knew when a coal or mineral train would reach its destination, trundling along happily until diverted to allow a passenger train to pass. Even though the signalmen were under strict instructions to get goods traffic out of the way of expresses, delays persisted.

Crews worked long hours, sometimes not moving through a single signal in a shift! No one could even start to know when consignments of coal or minerals would reach their destination. Six days was a common time for a coal run from Toton yard to London, while goods for export were held up by a lack of empty wagons for days, even weeks.

At this stage the Midland was taken in hand by a new and very remarkable General Manager, Guy Granet. Born in 1867 of wealthy parents, Granet was from a completely different background than earlier general managers. While Allport joined the B&DJ in a junior position and worked his way to the top, Guy Granet came in after an Oxford degree, the Bar and an introduction to railways as secretary of the Railway Companies' Association. A tall imposing figure, not often photographed, he had a most forceful personality, and never took previous practice as a sure guide, examining problems on their merits. Joining the Midland in 1905, first as deputy and then as general manager he found a railway in a mess.

Granet soon reorganised the Midland's organisation structure from top to bottom, giving his main attention to the operating departments. At the instigation of the newly-appointed locomotive superintendent, Cecil Paget, a centralised traffic control was set up to monitor the vast flows of goods and the streams of passenger traffic on the railway. Soon raised to the new high office of general superintendent, Paget set up a control system in a way which proved to be yet another successful Midland 'first'.

The control system and the locomotive power classification went hand-in-glove. Control was exercised initially through five offices at Cudworth, Toton, Masborough, Staveley and Westhouses, eventually extending to 26 centres.

'Control' would be able to make much more informed decisions than an isolated signalman about train movements. The insurance of this system was adopted first by the LMS after Grouping, then by British Railways. 'Control' also insisted on a rigid adherence to rules coupling the weight of trains to the capability of the locomotives assigned for the jobs. At the first sign of too many tons to pull, double-heading was ordered.

Double-headed: Unusual company for a Deeley 4-4-0 on the 10.00am Euston to Edinburgh at Carlisle was a locomotive from the former Caledonian Railway. Post-Grouping times saw strange bedfellows – even Claughtons were seen north of Leeds on 'Midland' metals after 1923 when they were displaced by Fowler Compounds from the West Coast Main Line. *L&GRP*.

Settle & Carlisle Goods: In one of the few photographs of Midland locomotives on the Settle & Carlisle line, 0-6-0 No 2914 pulls one of the thousands of goods trains to trundle over Ais Gill summit from the opening of the S&C in 1876. *L&GRP*.

Midland Goods Traffic

The Midland was very much a goods line. In 1875 for example, total passenger train mileage was only eight million; goods and mineral exceeded 14 million miles. Twenty years later goods and mineral trains ran for the incredible total of 25 million miles, when passenger train mileage was only 17 million. In the United Kingdom as a whole, passenger and goods traffic miles were evenly matched at around 100 million each in 1875, giving the Midland a substantial 14 per cent of the UK goods mileage—not bad for a one-time provincial line!

Goods were handled in extensive depots designed to allow loading and unloading horse-drawn waggons usually covered with exuberant advertisements for the owning line. In Manchester most goods were handled in a vast depot at Ancoats. London boasted no fewer than 28 goods depots, some capable of handling coal and cattle, spread over the Metropolis from Kew Bridge in the west to Poplar in the docks. The City Widened Lines were used to gain access to the tightly-knit rail system south of the Thames, with Midland Railway depots at Peckham and Wandsworth. There were no fewer than 38 receiving stations for goods and parcels in London by 1913, most placed in the Midland territory north-west of St Pancras.

Goods trains were made of rakes or 8- or 10-ton wagons pulled by 0-6-0s, usually trundling along at 15–20mph. Refuge sidings were provided every few miles to allow faster traffic to overtake. Until the traffic reforms of the late 1890s, such trains ran to no set time-table—no one knew when a coal train would reach Somers Town, Kew or Manchester. Some goods depots, such as that on the old Wicker station site in Sheffield, were congested and were kept going by miracles of improvisation. In rural areas many stations had a goods yard where wagons were shunted off or picked up, carrying all the infinite variety of merchandise for a farming community—fertiliser, machinery, clothes, food and livestock. It was not unusual for whole farms to be transported by train to a new start in the next county. On market days pandemonium reigned, with extra wagons ordered to cope with the cattle and sheep changing hands.

More valuable goods were carried by Class A goods trains running to set schedules at speeds of up to 35mph. Greater speed was not possible without fitted brakes on each wagon—time had to be allowed to brake gradually at junctions, and care was always taken to allow sufficient time for the poor brakes to operate to stop trains at signals. Acceleration was gradual, otherwise couplings broke, sometimes when speeding up at the top of a bank. Couplings were left tight to avoid snatching, with smart running downhill in case couplings would first sag and then break on pulling away up-hill. One typical run logged by *The Railway Magazine* in 1910 featured a Class A goods of 40 wagons, loaded to 12 tons each on a Somers Town to Bedford run. A Class 2F 0-6-0 covered the 6½ miles to Hendon in 17 minutes, Elstree in 31 minutes, and Radlett (15 miles) in 35 minutes. Switching to the slow road at Luton cost two minutes, made up by smart running down the bank to Bedford, reached in 98 minutes, for a 49-mile journey. Another goods run recorded, again in 1910, gave a Class 3F 0-6-0 pulling 500 tons to Bedford in 1 hour 43 minutes from Somers Town before taking the now defunct branch to Olney, where a Stratford-upon-Avon & Midland Junction Railway locomotive took over.

The goods carried by these trains was variable. All goods were classified to comply with Parliamentary maximum rates, set to reflect the value of goods and the care needed in transit. The variety of goods carried by train in Edwardian days can be judged from an extract from the *Classification Index* books held at every goods depot:

Goods	Class
Ore – chrome	C
– cobalt	3
– copper	C
– lead	C
– iron	A
– tin	1
– zinc	B
Organs – owner's risk	5
Ornaments – fireplace	3
– gypsum	5
– military (not plate)	3
– military (plate)	5
Osier twigs – wet	1
– stained	3
Osma burgs	2
Ovens	Special
Mowers	Special
Over-mantels – cast-iron	5
Oxalate of ammonia	Special

| Oxalate of potash | Special |
| Oxide of iron | C |

Each load would be costed by finding first its class and then a rate between the stations involved—usually set by Derby. Large loads were negotiable locally!

The volume of goods before World War I was immense – 67 million tons of general merchandise (12 million on the MR) in the whole of England in the peak year 1913. By 1933 this had dropped to 42 million tons; by 1983, when road competition had really taken its toll, this figure was only 10 million tons.

Midland Journeys in the 1890s

For the increasing number of people who could afford to take the train journeys were very different from those of today. A London to Nottingham passenger of 1890 (transported by a time machine to the 1980s) would be astonished by the speed of his HST 125, getting on for three times his staid 50mph in Midland days. The comfort of the second class would impress even the pampered Midland traveller, but the buffet food would do nothing for his Victorian appetite. At Nottingham he would be exasperated by the vast tracts of country beyond his reach by rail, at the long list of local services closed and abandoned—in his day only the most remote rural retreats were beyond the reach of a train.

In the 1980s scene most towns are served by only one line, whereas the earlier traveller would have been spoiled for choice, with two routes to Nottingham, (Midland or GN) and no fewer than three interwined lines up the Leen Valley. Even the great Midland stronghold of Derby had a GN station at Friargate. In 1890 Leicester enjoyed Midland and GN services, with the new Great Central coming in a few years later. Our 1890 traveller could choose between three routes to Manchester – Midland via Derby, LNWR via Crewe, or the GN and MS&L through Sheffield.

Reaching his destination, he took the horse bus to an hotel. Even quiet, small Wellingborough had a special bus for the 'Hind'. In London the Midland ran extensive services of buses to the termini of other lines. A traveller to the Continent could if he so desired change trains at Kentish Town and go on direct over the City Widened Lines to the Channel Ports without changing trains. Our 1880 friend would miss so many other things in 1987 – porters in profusion to help him with his copious baggage, beer available at the stations at any time, and he would be petrified by the prices of the 1980s . . .

Stations

The Midland system had ten major stations, St Pancras, Leicester, Derby, Nottingham, Sheffield, Leeds, Manchester, Carlisle, Bristol (Temple Meads) and Birmingham, the last four not owned uniquely by the Midland but under joint working arrangements. They were a varied lot: St Pancras and Manchester Central stood as monuments to High Victorian engineering, Temple Meads was one of Brunel's triumphs, but Leeds (Wellington) was ripe for pulling down in 1900 and remained in a sordid condition until replaced by Leeds City, built by BR.

The building of St Pancras has already been described; its character in the heyday of the Midland has been incomparably recalled by Alan Jackson. Never the busiest of the London termini, it could boast only 150 trains a day in 1902. Local trains worked to Moorgate, so one mercifully avoided the frantic chaos of Liverpool Street or the steady stream of city workers of Waterloo and London Bridge, The main line expresses departed at stately intervals for Manchester, Leeds, Bradford, Scotland and the Midlands. A variety of other companies also used the station, prior to grouping. The GER sent trains to Harwich and to Norwich via the Tottenham line until 1917, while the London, Tilbury & Southend used St Pancras as a 'West End' terminus. Before 1914 royal Sandringham-bound travellers via the GER entrained at St Pancras in preference to Liverpool Street, showing excellent perception! Travelling from St Pancras was always an 'experience', not a trial. In contrast Leeds (Wellington) was a disaster. However, many travellers from Leeds, especially the 'commercials', made good use of its murky facilities – the left luggage department was always full to overflowing with their samples. The busy staff of over 200 coped with a heavy load, as the six platforms sent trains to most of the manufacturing districts of the country, with excellent connections to the North, London and Bristol. The Leeds station master of 1904 was typical of his kind. Entering the Midland's service as a boy at Settle, he worked at Kettering, Derby and Morecambe before reaching the top post at Leeds.

Derby remained the well-appointed station built by the NMR until German bombs in World War II destroyed the platform areas. BR patched up things using concrete, and extensively rebuilding, sadly without retaining the magnificent Thompson frontage. Nottingham was not so well endowed by the MCR, the Midland eventually rebuilding the station in 'High Midland' style in 1904. An overbridge led down to five long curved platforms, marred by the girders of the Great Central Line going right across. The fine Midland buildings, with a clock tower, remain, serving passengers by an excellent HST service to St Pancras in under two hours. The rival Nottingham Victoria station built at enormous expense by the Great Central Railway has been replaced by a shopping precinct, but 'Midland' is now being refurbished.

Leicester, London Road, was Midland-built near the old MCR Campbell Street site. Now, again rebuilt by BR, it is a fitting successor to the elegant Midland station, retaining the basic plan of overbridge and easy platform access, and the fine late Victorian entrance.

New Street, Birmingham, was built by the LNWR to relieve the poorly-sited Curzon Street terminus, left down the hill beyond the Bull Ring, in a maze of small streets. New Street station was brought into use on 1 June 1854 with a banquet and other marks of an important railway event. All the LNWR services to and from Curzon Street station were transferred to the new station, but Midland trains continued to use the old terminus until 30 June.

The 'Midland started to use New Street gradually; to mid-1885 expresses went via the old line through Camp Hill, with portions detached for New Street. Then the tunnel beyond New Street, to Church Road Junction was built, the Western Suburban line was doubled to Stirchley Street, and a new station opened at Five Ways. From 1 October 1885 expresses ran via New Street and King's Norton. After intermingling of Midland and LNWR expresses, soon Midland trains had their own platforms. Curzon Street, used for excursion traffic until 1893, became a goods station and suffered the deprivations of neglect. Curzen Street is now a finely restored building, housing offices for the Birmingham area job creation organisation, its hall graced by a well presented display of photographs from London & Birmingham and B&DJR days. No one could have loved the old New Street, with its draughts and rambling ill-lit passageways. The author prefers its replacement with its easy access to the centre of Birmingham, frequent London service and cross-platform connections from trains on the old Midland West Country main line to Manchester and Scotland.

Carlisle Citadel is the well named gateway to Scotland. A stop there still evokes memories of pre-Grouping glories when seven companies used it. Built by the LNWR and the Caledonian, the Midland had right of entry under the Settle & Carlisle Act, paying rent to the owners. These worthies enlarged the station in 1880, retaining the old main platform (long overloaded by the traffic pouring through), adding a large island platform and five bays for the many local trains terminating or starting at Carlisle. The $6\frac{1}{2}$-acre glass roof had vast end glass walls, seen in thousands of photographs of trains leaving Citadel.

David Joy in his history *The Railways of the Lake Counties* has told of the character of Citadel, the stately Midland Pullmans, the LNWR Scotch expresses, the locals to Maryport, the NER trains to Newcastle, the sheer diversity of the seven pre-Grouping railways that regularly steamed in and out of this great station.

Sheffield Midland still thrives, with busy services to Manchester and the North-East to South-West HST 125s. This friendly station, the author's favourite, also has a good InterCity 125 London service, unfortunately slowed down by the need to divert to Nottingham or Derby instead of coming straight down the Erewash Valley to London. Outlasting the MS&L Victoria station, Sheffield Midland is

The fine and typically Midland ironwork at Kettering station

a neat tidy place, still retaining a faint aura of the Midland at its greatest. In contrast, over the Pennines, Manchester Central, the old CLC terminus—once a fine station, built like St Pancras but with poor, wooden offices—is now an exhibition centre.

Intermediate stations on the Midland, like Kettering or Rother-ham, were always well built and usually placed nearer to the centre of town than their rivals. Kettering still stands four-square, an easy walk from the town, with four ample sweeping platforms covered with characteristic fine glass roofs. The offices are small but soundly built, with a small refreshment room-cum-bookstall; the passenger under-pass harks back to its Victorian origins, and is suitable only for a scene from a 'Jack the Ripper' film. Rotherham is built to a similar design, but is far less convenient for the town. Many of these intermediate stations are giving good service today and will stand as long as trains run.

So also stand the smaller Midland stations, though sadly many have taken the toll of closure. Typical of the small Midland station is Settle, with its compact offices on one platform, looking as much part of the Pennines as the old town it serves, but its service is sparse and under threat. These small Midland stations were built to last! Not for the Midland the shiplap board of the London Brighton & South Coast, or the jerry building of the Chatham. The Midland built for a harsh climate and built for posterity. Fortunately for us, a typical small station has been preserved at Ripley by the Midland Railway Trust and another by the Worth Valley Railway Line, encapsulated on film in *The Railway Children*.

Working in a country station in the steam age was not at all placid. The small staff of stationmaster, helped by two porters each shift had plenty to do besides being on hand to attend to trains. The rural station was the sole route for goods in and out of its community, so quantities of manufactures would be handled each week, balanced by products of the farms around the station. An old porter at Ulles-thorpe, on the original MCR line from Leicester to Rugby, tells how four local pick-up goods trains called at this country station daily, two each way between Leicester and Rugby. Up to fifty 10-ton wagons would be detached in a week, all unloaded by the staff, with goods for the local timber yard as well as the numerous local farms, each sending milk away and receiving fertiliser and cattle feed. All local train shunting was done by the porters, lamps serviced, trains seen away, timber labelled and checked, as well as loading and sheeting it on wagons. There could be as many as 22 transfer orders on one truck, all to be recorded, checked and issued to the waiting merchants or farmers. On top of this, livestock was always on the move by rail in those days, with the attendant cleaning chores! Then, when all this was finished the station was cleaned and was polished bright by the poor, hard-working porters.

Midland Hotels

The wealthy traveller on the Midland was cosseted on his journey from beginning to end. Cabs and omnibuses abounded to take him onwards from the station, and if he chose he could stay at one of the magnificent hotels operated by the company. Pride of place was taken by the Midland Grand Hotel at St Pancras, operated to the highest international standards of comfort and service. The Midland Hotel at Derby, the first railway hotel in the world, still gives a good night's stay close to the station. The Company also operated hotels at Liverpool (The Adelphi), at Leeds (the Queen's), at Morecambe and at Manchester, where the Midland Hotel still has five-star rooms right in the city centre.

This last hotel, opened in 1903, caused *The Railway Magazine* to eulogise 'an enterprise which when contempleted is a temptation to credit the word – Midland – with some magic.' The magazine's correspondent, full of praise for the new standard of hotel-keeping in the provinces, was full of praise also for the manager over all the Midland's Hotels, William Towle. Overlord of 1,900 staff, he had evidently surpassed himself at Manchester where, designed by the company architect Charles Trubshaw, the Midland was built right in the centre of town on the site of the old people's concert hall!

Large for its day, with 500 rooms, the Midland Hotel, Manchester, possessed only 100 baths, provision lavish for the time. Of renaissance style, the exterior was covered in terracotta to diminish the effects of the Manchester grime. A series of linen filters was used to trap that same grime before it could enter the hotel. A roof garden allowed its lucky patrons to look down, breathing filtered air, onto the pall of smog so common in turn-of-century Manchester. A great ballroom, decorated in Louis XIV style, was soon used to house some of the concerts so well patronised by Mancunians. Visitors could choose between French and German restaurants, before sleeping in bedrooms each fitted with a telephone. Even in those days some rooms had their own bathroom!

The Midland, once the flagship of the group, still serves travellers well, with a five-star rating and the same gastronomic flair. Its customers can no longer travel on the Midland, many arriving by car or plane, but it still aims to surround travellers in luxury redolent of Edwardian elegance. St Pancras, sadly ceased taking guests in the 1930s—it found itself too far from the West End and too near the Pentonville Road for comfort.

Midland Food

Victorian railway journeys went at a leisurely pace, so the stout eaters of the day became much in need of sustenance. James Allport, conscious of their needs solved the problem of feeding whole trainloads in the pre-refreshment car era by building extensive refreshment rooms at Normanton. The early Midland Scotch expresses stopped there for 30 minutes, time enough for a meal and attention to other basic needs. There were daily scenes of chaos and panic as hungry trainloads descended on the single counter of the island platform dining room, devouring the early version of the railway sandwich or, for the more affluent, a rapidly taken three-course meal. In 1882 the Midland introduced eating facilities on the early Scotch expresses in the Pullman dining coaches, serving meals at each first class passenger's seat. Later in the 1890s magnificent corridor stock was introduced with dining cars for both first and third classes. Many wise passengers continued to circumnavigate the Normanton chaos or the Leeds scramble by taking their own food with them—wealthier ones bought railway hampers, stuffed with cold chicken, fruit cake, wine, and so on.

By 1903 the Midland proudly advertised first and third class breakfast, luncheon and dining cars on all the 16 main departures from St Pancras. Some trains to and from Bristol were also equipped with dining cars, one going on as far as Bradford and Leeds. Breakfast was half-a-crown (£0.12½), dinner three shillings and sixpence (£0.17½), three shillings (£0.15) in third class. The minimum meal was a steak or chop, with vegetables, sweets and cheese. Luncheon baskets, hot or cold, were available at all the main stations to help passengers travelling on in through-carriages to foreign lines, such as the L&YR, not well favoured with diners. In the affluent, leisured years of the mature Midland, food was used to good effect as a most potent inducement to entice passengers away from the Euston or King's Cross rivals.

Midland Style

Every pre-grouping railway company had a distinctive house style and the Midland was no exception. Solid and luxurious were the underlying tenets of the style which was used in every part of the system from Bath to Carlisle. Nothing was shoddy, buildings were stoutly made from local materials. Uniforms were well made, carriages and locomotives painted in rich colours to keep their gloss despite the gloom and dirt of steam lines in the industrial heartland of England.

Midland stations were built four-square and solid with a clear style. Common features of station details were the iron lattice windows with lozenge patterns and a profusion of barge boards. On some main line stations a Wyvern, the Midland emblem, was placed, executed in stone and prominently displayed. On Sheffield Midland it can be seen still, but the famous Derby example has gone with redevelopment. Medium-sized stations like Kettering had a distinctive form of platform glass roofing inspired by Paxton of Crystal Palace fame. Notices and timetables boards were all in a clear house style, well lettered, leaving no doubt as to the ownership.

Signalboxes and signal design altered little from the earliest days. Several have survived well protected by their slate roofs, like the example at Settle Junction. A typical box had a hipped roof over a stout wooden construction, with vertical boards to the floor level and horizontal ones to the ground. Glazing was usually to floor level with the name of the box clearly displayed below window level. The main structure was always in lemon chrome, with handrails and other details in venetian red, but with window frames in white. Inside, brown lino covered the floor, contrasting with the bright colour-coded signal levers and the profusion of well-polished brass telegraph instruments. Outside, signals were equally distinctive; lower quadrant semaphores on stout square wooden posts surmounted by filials shaped like a German soldier's *pickelhaube*! Signal posts were painted in the same chrome as the signalboxes, usually maturing to a stone colour in the industrial grime. Signalboards were a shade of red, called Markeaton red after the Derby firm supplying it.

All Midland station employees wore uniform, changing in keeping with their status. Stationmasters in the important cities like Leeds, Sheffield and Derby wore a top hat and frock coat, one of many Midland 'firsts' which has survived in a modified form even to this day. Other stationmasters wore a cap like a French *gendarme*'s, but rather flatter, with the grade of station denoted by the colour (gold or silver) of the braid round the cap. All wore frock coats, a Wyvern cap

155

badge with the letters MR on the front of the cap. Guards also wore frock coats with military caps, heavily silver-braided for those on the major expresses. Goods guards were not so splendid, but in keeping with all grades in sight of the public, they wore a good quality uniform in keeping with the prosperity and stability of the company.

The famous 'Midland Red' locomotive colour was not introduced until 1883. Designated 'oxide of iron' this crimson-lake colour became the universal mark of a Midland locomotive, resplendent with the letters MR on buffers and tenders. Distinctive and elegant numbers were painted on the cabsides, but names (with the exception of two locomotives *Princess of Wales* and *Beatrice*) were not used. In the last of the many minor variations in locomotive painting style the company arms were placed on the driving wheel splashers and the locomotive number painted in prominent numerals on the tender, a habit carried into LMS days.

The Derby locomotive painting specification was subject to a certain degree of interpretation by the painters at Kentish Town, where the superintendent, Mr Weatherburn, was allowed some local liberty. He used a slightly deeper shade of red and favoured numerous minor deviations from the Derby canon, giving Midland enthusiasts many happy hours looking for these on photographs of locomotives of the 1880s. The Spinners were especially rich in 'Weatherburns.' Bristol and Leeds sheds played similar jolly games—with what horror would they be regarded by the conformist managers of today!

Coaches were also magnificently got up in red, with lettering denoting class at the waist and 'Midland' near roof height. Diners or sleeping cars were so lettered at waist level, using very distinctive lettering.

Accidents

In his book *Red for Danger*, a lucid and comprehensive account of railway accidents in Great Britain and Ireland, L.T.C. Rolt lists only one on the Midland lines up to 1880. Before then Midland trains ran in all weathers with commendable safety despite increasing traffic, faster speeds, the almost complete lack of safety equipment and a chronic absence of braking power. The speed-up started by John Noble destroyed this good record completely; within six months of August 1880 seven serious accidents hit the Midland. From then on the Midland safety record continued to be excellent, marred only by major news-catching disasters in 1898, 1910 and 1911. The worst of the 1880 accidents occurred at Manchester in September, when the

Brute force: The 1 in 37 Lickey Bank, near Bromsgrove on the Gloucester to Birmingham Line, needed every ounce of muscle to push the frequent heavy goods trains up towards Birmingham. Built in 1919, No 2290, the one and only giant 0-10-0 banker was nicknamed 'Big Bertha' after the gun used in World War I. No 2290 was tried unsuccessfully on Toton – Cricklewood coal trains before the LMS ordered the massive 2-6-0+0-6-2 Beyer Garratts. No 2290 was withdrawn in 1956. *L&GRP*.

Accident at Wellingborough: In 1898 a GPO porter allowed a trolley to run onto the track as the 7.15pm St Pancras to Manchester diner thundered through Wellingborough at speed. This photograph shows the aftermath, in which five passengers and the enginemen perished. *L&GRP*.

driver of new 2-4-0 No 1295 became over-confident of his locomotive's steam brakes and of the Sanders automatic vacuum brakes fitted to all the carriages. The 9.00am Liverpool to St Pancras called at Manchester Central before travelling south over the Peak line to Derby and London. Central was normally approached slowly, but on 2 September repairs called for a dead-slow traverse of the reverse curves into the station. Driver Salmon over-estimated the stopping power of his brakes and ran into the curves at too high a speed, causing No 1295 to jump a set of facing points, demolishing the station signal box, whose occupant had just jumped out, saving his life.

Within months, tragedy struck the Midland again, at Leeds Wellington station. Just before Christmas 1880 the station was full of traffic. On the last market day before the holiday, extra carriages were needed for the 5.30pm 'stopper' to Sheffield. The train engine, a new 2-4-0 was used to fetch three extras, but one was not needed and drawn clear. The train left, full to overflowing, ten minutes late, but only after driver Stone reminded the relief signalman of his presence and need to get on the road. The bobby, instead of giving the 'all clear' by a signal, waved a white light to allow the train to leave. Driver Stone was puzzled and got confirmation of the road from a foreman on the platform. To his horror Stone realised, only after leaving the station well behind, that he was on the wrong line. Soon the lights of the 2.55pm ex Derby were upon him and a terrible collision took place. At the official inquiry the inspection officer, Major Marindin, found that the unfortunate relief signalman was to blame. The unwanted coach had fouled a pair of facing points, so preventing the 'bobby' from pulling off the starting signal. The unfortunate relief man then allowed the train to proceed, not noticing that points were set for the wrong line.

In 1880 the Midland staff were suffering under the strain of the new timetables introduced earlier that year. Established routines were changed, speeds improved and new timings had to be learned. The result was a whole range of lesser disasters, adding up to a terrible year for the hitherto safe and sure line. Soon things settled down and passengers got used to the safe, sure passage of their well-appointed trains, with only minor accidents to mar an excellent safety record. However, in the early autumn of 1898 a real pile-up occured at Wellingborough due to the carelessness of a GPO porter, who had left his trolley on the up platform without properly immobilising it. The vehicle, left only for a few seconds, rolled across the platform onto the track and despite the frantic efforts of station staff was hit by the 7.15pm dining car express from St Pancras, thundering through the station at 60mph. The express 4-4-0 was derailed on the diamond crossing at the north end of the station, killing the crew and reducing the six carriages to a tangled mess. Five passengers also died and most of the remaining 60 passengers were injured. Bad as it was, the real tragedy of Wellingborough was the unheeded warning in the inspector's report saying 'Carriage No 3002 took fire in consequence of an escape of gas from the cylinder underneath the carriage.' In this simple statement lay a major disaster waiting, lurking unheeded down the years.

A lesser disaster occurred in 1905 near Cudworth when a Leeds to London night express, with Scotch sleepers attached, ran into a slow-moving mail train, also from Leeds. Only prompt action in protecting the line saved a really monumental pile-up. Eighteen months later fog resulted in another collision at Tapton, south of Sheffield. An 0-6-0 struck an old Kirtley 0-6-0 then standing on the up passenger line after service on a ballast train. A third light engine was damaged in this accident, caused by the local signalman's inattention, compounded by lack of safety aids—even simple track circuiting would have helped the 'bobby' who may well have done a 12-hour stint in the darkness and fog.

Disaster on the Moors

The danger lurking under every Midland carriage throughout the 1880s and 1890s, lighting gas, found its mark at last in 1910 on the most exposed part of the Settle to Carlisle line at a point where a branch from Hawes joined the S&C. Hawes Junction, later Garsdale was an isolated spot, windswept and cold in summer, in winter bleak beyond belief. The station yard had a turntable, protected by a stockade against the gales blowing from the moors. The yard at the junction was busy night and day with the many pilot engines freed from assisting the heavy expresses up the gradients from Carlisle or Settle. The 'small engine' policy of the Midland ensured that most passenger trains and many goods needed piloting up the banks to the summit near to Hawes Junction. This activity went on day and night; the signalman at the junction had numerous movements of light engines to control, some across the yard, others up to the turntable and back down the grades for another train to bank over the roof of England.

On Christmas Eve 1910 things were extra busy with traffic still rushing through the junction, most trains needing a banker. In the darkness the rain poured down from the moors making visibility difficult. All the 'bobby' could see were the lights of locomotives, dimly through his windows. At one time he had no fewer than five light engines on his hands, two of which, coupled together ready to go back down the long descent to Carlisle, were standing on the down main line. At 5.23am while the driver of a light engine turned it, he noticed two Class A goods come through on the up line, then the down main line signals came off and the Carlisle locomotives moved forward slowly. The time was 5.44am in the worst period before the dawn. The watching driver saw to his horror that the signals were not returned to danger to protect the light engines, which were ambling down the road to home. Within a moment the midnight St Pancras to Glasgow sleeper roared through the station, followed within minutes by sound of an alarm whistle left on and on, shrieking across the dark moors from the north.

Near Grisedale crossing, on the Carlisle side of Morcock Tunnel, the sleeper had ploughed straight into the light engines, vainly trying to accelerate away from the express bearing down out of the dark tunnel. Most of the express train was fitted with Pintsch oil gas lighting stored at a pressure of 65lb/sq in, so on impact many of the sleeping passengers were incinerated. The toll could have been worse, but twelve people were killed, and several seriously injured. The inquiry showed that the signalman at Hawes Junction, preoccupied in passing the two up goods, had forgotten the light engines, but their drivers had also ignored Rule 55, not reminding the signalman of their presence. The government inspecting officer recommended the installation of track circuiting at the busy Midland Junction to remind the signalman of locomotives standing at signals. This new device would have saved the lives of the passengers who died on the moors in the blazing train. The signalman had been on duty for ten hours, all through a busy night, with no aids to remind him of the presence of trains, not even a collar for the levers. The wonder is that many more accidents did not occur due to the lack of simple equipment to assist signalmen and drivers. The inspecting officer once again reminded the Midland of the dangers of gas lighting but the board took no notice.

Within three years the Hawes Junction disaster was repeated, again on the Settle to Carlisle line, at Ais Gill summit. In the autumn of 1913, driver Nicholson was working the 1.35am sleeper ex Carlisle over the moors with 4-4-0 No 993. The limit for this locomotive over the S&C was 430 tons, but that night the train was 13 tons over weight, with no pilot available. Normally this would be a manageable load for the locomotive, but Durranhill shed had supplied coal with a great deal of 'fines'. Steaming, even with the experienced driver firing, was almost impossible. Above Kirkby Stephen the steam pressure dropped and the locomotive slowed down to a crawl as the vacuum brakes leaked. At 2.57am the train halted just below Ais Gill summit. Meanwhile, the 1.49am Carlisle had left the border city on time, the lighter load of 157 tons well within the limit of the Class 2 4-4-0 in charge. The injector on the Class 2 was giving trouble and both driver and fireman were preoccupied in coaxing it back into service – in only four minutes' wrestling with the injector the train ran through all the signals at Mallerstang. This was well before the days of audible warning of signals in the cab and the crew had no idea of the danger ahead. With the injector working, they looked up but it was too late! The fireman gasped as he saw the red lights of the stalled train in front, but no amount of emergency braking could save a collision. The Class 2 ploughed into the stalled train at 45mph, the brake van coming to rest in a third class carriage at the rear of the front train. The results were hideous as fire broke out quickly from gas ignited by red-hot coals. Fourteen passengers were burned to death, and 38 injured.

These two disasters occurring at night, lit up by the glow of fires roaring through the crashed trains so quickly that escape was impossible, raised public concern about the wisdom of travelling on the Midland.

In the life remaining to it, the Midland was free of further disasters – thanks only to the unceasing vigilance of its staff, working without benefit of the many safety measures now used on railways in Britain.

Finale—The War and Grouping

No observer looking at Britain in 1912 could have foreseen the enormous changes of the next ten years. Within the decade World War I would completely change the whole pattern of life for better or worse, depending on one's point of view. After the war, years of poor maintenance and of rising costs would lead to a major railway amalgamation, destroying the identities of all but one of the pre-Grouping lines, replacing them by mammoth organisations, racked by the problems of size.

Back in 1912 our observer would notice one surprising change—the Midland takeover of the London, Tilbury & Southend lines. It had been known for some time that the LT&S was ready for absorption by a major railway, with the GE as the natural contender. History in the guise of the Gloucester lines 70 or so years earlier repeated itself, and the Midland was faster on its feet, securing the LT&S for £240 of 2½ per cent preference stock for each £100 of Tilbury stock. As a consolation prize the Great Eastern secured running powers into St Pancras in return for extending Fenchurch Street terminus and widening its approaches. The LT&S was never completely 'Midlandised'—its trains were quoted in Bradshaw separately as 'Midland—LTS section'; Derby went no further than providing some new 4-4-2 tanks for the intensive services.

The Great War brought irreversible changes to the railways of Britain. Run by the wartime Railway Executive Committee all the lines, Midland included, passed quickly under Government control. Each was given a payment based on the net receipts for 1913, but was constrained to charge civilian passengers and freight rates at their pre-war levels. These restrictions started a major decline in the fortunes of all the old companies and led to the amalgamation of 1923.

All Midland excursion traffic was cancelled in 1914, steamer sailings to the Isle of Man and Belfast were drastically cut, and paths for the huge movement of munitions and troops made available by a sharp reduction in express services. Troop specials sometimes overwhelmed the system, as when Luton was besieged by no fewer than 132 special trains over one weekend! The REC in its infinite wisdom decided that the Midland was a 'goods' line, cutting most of the Leeds and Manchester expresses from St Pancras. The Midland never recovered this traffic, which was lost to Crewe and Doncaster.

By 1917 all these measures had bitten deep into the Midland's services and the overcrowded trains were running at only half the pre-war mileage. The long-distance trains were seriously overcrowded. The Settle to Carlisle line now suffered the most serious dislocation to services anywhere on the system as an endless procession of government specials shouldered the regular services aside carrying coal and naval stores to Scotland and to Scapa Flow.

The puny Midland locomotives gave their best with the huge loads. Class 2s normally limited to 180 tons were capable when pushed of taking double that weight up the Lickey bank and the 'Drag'. Examples of valiant efforts abounded, due to the excellence of Midland maintenance and to severe speed restrictions imposed on account of economical coal consumption.

The old Class 1 passenger locomotives, the venerable Kirtley 2-4-0s, and the singles were pressed into pilot duties on coal trains leaving Toton for Portsmouth or Scapa Flow. Many times an elegant

HIGH MIDLAND: A GREAT RAILWAY

Johnson single was seen piloting an ancient Kirtley 0-6-0 up the line to Leeds and beyond.

Munitions were needed in quantities not dreamed of before, the Midland serving no fewer than 97 new munition factories set up after 1912. Longbridge, now a centre of motor manufacture, became a mighty factory for aero engines, guns and shells. The Midland took 12,000 workers in and out of Longbridge from central Birmingham daily. From Warmley 10 million hand grenades, from Earby 90,000 tons of explosives, from Manchester 80,000 tons of iron castings— these were typical of the monumental traffic carried by the Midland in the Great War. The Chilwell National Shell Factory was served by special Midland sidings laid out near Nottingham, adding to the congestion in this Nottingham—Trent area. Derby works was given over to war effort almost entirely, turning out 7½ million renovated cartridge cases, 2½ million complete fuses, 1½ million fuse adapters, 25,000 gun mountings, 40 tank conveyors, 4,500 aircraft, and countless parts for aircraft, armoured cars and tanks.

The human cost in the war was also great. With over 20,000 men from the railway in the forces, the burden was carried by those remaining, while over a third of those who joined the Colours never returned, an enormous loss in terms of experience and human tears.

The Midland's services never recovered fully from the effects of the war. In 1922 just before Grouping, there were only three day and three night trains to Scotland, compared with a total of nine in 1910. The 1922 timings were slower than those of 1910 and compared badly with the rival west and east coast trains.

Manchester had become an LNWR preserve and the Midland's grip on its 'home' towns was threatened by smart GC timings to Marylebone. Leeds was a 4½-hour trip by Midland, four hours by GN, but the departures from London by these two old rivals were decently staggered with the King's Cross trains leaving at 7.15am, 10.10am and 1.30pm. St Pancras-Leeds services left at 9.00am, 11,30am and 3.30pm. Altogether the Midland had lost its sharp competitive edge of 1910, and was still wedded to the small locomotive policy at a time when the LNWR and the GN had the beginnings of a fleet of more powerful locomotives. The line was devoid of six-coupled express types just when the needs of modern railways were dictating a switch to 4-6-0s and pacifics. In the early 1920s when the GWR was designing the Castle class 4-6-0s, with large boilers and good valve events, the Midland was still building 19th Century locomotives. Well designed though they were, with superbly tried and tested components, well in advance of all but GWR practice, Midland

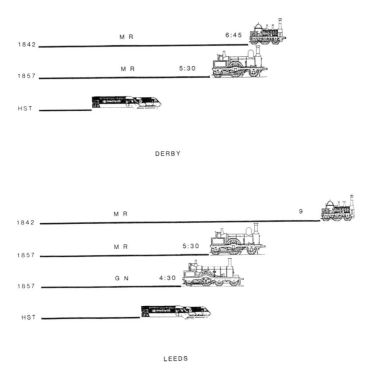

The changing pattern of speed on the Midland main line down the years

locomotives were just too small. Brakes, valves and lubrication were all first class; it was the overall concept of an adequately powered modern locomotive that was lacking.

By 1921 it was evident to most railwaymen and to the government that the railway system in Britain was grinding to a halt. The war years under the twin handicap of an enormous volume of traffic and the sheer lack of maintenance had reduced the whole system to a crawl. So in 1921 the Government passed the Railways Act, precipitating four shotgun marriages of all the sizeable lines. There emerged four groups, based on the old railways rather than any idea of a geographical grouping of lines. Only the GWR retained its identity, the LSWR joining the LBSCR and SECR as the Southern Railway. The GN was teamed with the NER and Scottish lines as the London & North Eastern Railway. The biggest of the grouped railways was made up of the Midland, the recently amalgamated LNWR and L&Y, the 'Caley', the 'Sou' West', along with smaller lines such as the Furness and the North Staffs. The massive new railway, stretching from the far North of Scotland to Bournemouth, was called the London, Midland & Scottish. This, the largest joint stock railway company in the world, started life on New Year's Day 1923. Its crest sported the Wyvern of the Midland, at the top, overlooking the emblems of Scotland and England. This symbolism was prophetic—the Midland reigned supreme in the new line, over its old rivals, the North Western and the 'Caley'.

9

LONDON MIDLAND & SCOTTISH

The formation of the LMS, on 1 January 1923 saw one of the biggest amalgamations ever in the business field. At a stroke the largest joint stock railway in the world came into being, whose track ran from the deep south of England to the farthest north of Scotland, from the East Midlands right across to West Wales. The first, the second and the fifth largest of the old companies, in terms of net receipts, combined into one corporate body possessing a fleet in excess of 10,000 locomotives. Welding together the constituent companies, large railways in their own right. was no easy task, especially as the new company was subject to one of the fundamental rules of amalgamations: 'In any amalgamation one constituent always comes out on top'.

In the early years of the LMS the top party was the Midland. Until the new railway was at least ten years old Midland ideas prevailed and ex-Midland officers dominated the company, sometimes to good effect, sometimes to bad. Midland dominance started with the composition of the first board, selected by the 1923 Railways Act from the old companies in proportion to their company's capital. The Midland was worth £160 million at formation, the LNWR and L&Y £120 million each, the others rather less, so the LMS had eight former Midland directors, six each from the LNWR and the L&Y and one each from the Furness, the G&SW, and the Highland. The Caley and the North Staffs were not represented until later owing to a dispute concerning compensation.

Although the LMS chairman was a North Western man, the dominant force on the board was the former Midland General Manager, the redoubtable Sir Guy Granet. As a deputy chairman, distinguished in World War I as the overlord of the vital military rail links in France, Granet was in a commanding position to ensure that the new railway was run on Midland lines. The all-important chief officers of the new line were: General Manager - Arthur Watson, LYR; Chief General

'Black Five': No book which includes the Midland lines in LMS days would be complete without a photograph of a 'Black Five'. This rather grubby specimen was seen on the Somerset & Dorset main line pulling a rake of LMS coaches, with their distinctly Midland look. The ubiquitous Class 5 mixed-traffic locomotives were superbly designed by Stanier, using his Swindon 'know how' coupled with Midland detail design skills. *L&GRP*.

Ancient and Modern: This fine photograph taken at Derby shows a classic goods 0-6-0 of the ultra-reliable Class 4F design, alongside an InterCity HST125 set. The locomotive was built to Fowler's Midland designs immediately after Grouping, so is not included on Midland lists. The 125 sets were built at Litchurch Lane to the highest standards, with the latest modern equipment. *Derby Evening Telegraph*.

Superintendent - J. H. Follows, MR; Goods Manager - S. Hunt, LNWR; Chief Mechanical Engineer - G. Hughes, L&YR.

A quick glance at this list is deceptive; in fact the key post was that of the Chief General Superintendent, J. H. Follows, who had occupied Granet's chair on the Midland during the war. Follows ran the LMS, and he ran it on Midland lines. Out were the days of Claughtons fighting their way North pulling a colossal weight of cars, diners and sleepers—in was the Midland system of closely regulated engine loads, with double-heading where necessary. The man who oversaw the running of the vast new locomotive fleet was the Superintendent of Motive Power, Anderson, the powerful former Midland Deputy CME. He saw to it that true Midland principles ruled supreme and that 'North Western' ideas were kept severely in their place—out of sight! On the locomotive design side, Hughes was near to retirement and his deputy, Fowler of the Midland, knighted for his war efforts, was well placed to keep Midland ideas well to the fore.

The new railway soon adopted the Midland livery, which was no bad thing. Crimson lake had proved itself to be an attractive and economical colour, which lasted to the end of the LMS in 1947. Basic train services remained largely unchanged at first, although there were moves behind the scenes towards the Midland concept of frequent, lightly-loaded trains.

Midland dominance was reinforced in 1924 by the retirement of the ex LNWR chairman, with the redoubtable and forceful Sir Guy Granet taking over. This superb organiser and manager built up the new LMS top organisation in a skilful and constructive way, sowing the seeds for the future greatness of the railway. Two years later, with his retirement looming, Granet brought in another powerful figure, Sir Josiah Stamp, as President of the Executive. The new managing committee was to run the LMS with skill and flair, (later adding to its number a true son of Swindon, William Stanier). The first Vice-Presidents, under the new régime were: J. H. Follows - railway traffic operating; S. H. Hunt - commercial; John Quirey - accounting and service departments; R. W. Reid - works and ancillary undertakings.

These were all bar Hunt, good Midland men and true! Reid was a notable Midland carriage and waggon superintendent in the Clayton mould, who also included locomotive design in his bailiwick. Midland operating ideas were firmly followed, central control, strict regulation of loads *à la* Paget, no more Claughtons straining under huge loads. Inevitably there was resistance, led by the Crewe guerillas and the Horwich brigade, with Reid discovering that engineers are incredibly conservative souls.

So in the field of locomotive design were drawn the battle lines within the new company—Crewe versus Derby. Beames, the old Crewe manager, was pushed aside and Claughtons and the Princes demoted to secondary duties. All was Midland, compounds and double-heading galore, but eventually, Swindon ways triumphed and the LMS was able at last to have a fleet of powerful and efficient locomotives fit for their varied purposes, the west coast mainline expresses, the long coal trains winding their way along the vast spider's web of LMS lines stretching from Thurso to Bournemouth!

Locomotives – The Early Years

George Hughes of the Lancashire & Yorkshire Railway was appointed Chief Mechanical Engineer of the new LMS, with Fowler as Deputy. He inherited 10,316 locomotives of many varied designs from works with widely differing views on the design of steam locomotives. The picture was well summed up by an old Derby man saying:

At Derby the nice little engines were made pets of. They were housed in nice clean sheds and were very lightly loaded. There must have been a Society for the Prevention of Cruelty to Engines in existence. At Horwich they had gone all scientific and talked in 'thous,' although apparently some of their work was to the nearest half-inch. At Crewe they just didn't care so long as the engines could roar and rattle along with a good paying load, which they usually did!

By 1923 Collett of the GWR had clearly established the main features of good locomotive design and had built in the Castles, the best-ever classic Stephenson steam locomotive, using a large super-heated boiler, clear steam passages and long valve travel. Nevertheless, despite the GWR lead, the new LMS main works—Derby, Crewe, Horwich, St Rollox—was each utterly convinced that its designs were the only one suited to its own lines and conditions. Few locomotives turned out by these works were based on the basic Churchward precepts, which only spread in later years, when Swindon engineers moved to high office in other railways.

Swindon was not having things all its own way, and the LMS works had built some excellent locomotives. An impartial observer, like the Horwich-trained E. S. Cox (later a deputy CME of British Rail) thought very highly of Derby designs, especially the 45 compounds

169

built before grouping. They were of a simple and reliable design, giving good service on the light trains of the pre-1914 era. They were free from the many faults of the LNWR Claughtons. Maintenance costs were low and they had a very real advantage in a 20 per cent lower coal consumption than rival designs. Until the larger LMS locomotives came along, 195 were built, doing sterling work until the end of steam.

Nevertheless the new railway lacked powerful, express locomotives with the capabilities of the Castles. Also lacking were large passenger tanks and powerful freight locomotives for the long coal hauls. Good mixed-traffic locomotives similar to those developed by Urie of the LSWR were also in short supply.

Hughes set about his new tasks in a most orderly and systematic manner, worthy of Horwich at its best, collecting comparative performance data on all the locomotive types inherited by the new line. Hughes was also in touch with the development in America and in France.

He put all his experience and his newly-acquired detailed knowledge of comparative locomotive performance to good effect by designing a first class mixed-traffic Class 5 2-6-0, the 'Crab,' of which 245 were built at Horwich and Derby. First out-shopped in 1926, they were a real advance in locomotive design, but revolutionary in appearance. The 21in cylinders were steeply inclined, involving a very high running plate. Smaller cylinders were ruled out by Hughes' dedication to the moderate boiler pressure of 180 lb/sq.in. He did change valve gears, using the best American practice in outside Walschaert motion—robust and easy to maintain.

Apart from this Horwich design, the LMS locomotive building policy up to 1926 was firmly Derby, due no doubt to the overwhelming Midland influence in the higher echelons of the new railway's management. Numbers tell the story: Of the 485 new locomotives built by the LMS from 1923 to 1925, 135 were Midland Compound 4-4-0s, 172 were superheated Midland 0-6-0s and 50 were the useful ex Midland shunting tanks! Only 78 locomotives were built to designs inherited from the other companies, mainly Horwich Baltic tanks or the LNWR Class 7 Crewe tanks. 'Non-standard' meant 'non-Derby'—only one real LNWR locomotive got through the Midland net!

The predominance of the Midland compounds in their superheated version over the old LNWR designs, the Claughtons and Princes, was not just due to weight of Midland influence in the corridors of power. Carefully conducted dynamometer car tests were carried out during

1923–1925 with the compounds and rival express types, notably the Caledonian 4-4-0s, the Claughtons and the Princes. The Settle to Carlisle line was the main venue, with the demanding S&D main line and the Preston to Carlisle routes used on some occasions. The compounds came out best from the tests, with coal consumption around 4lb/dbhp against their rivals' usual 5 lb/dbhp. These tests sealed the fate of the Claughtons. However, the 1925 publication of tests on a Castle quoting coal burnt at only 2.83 lb/dbhp was a sign of things to come. The compounds were entering their last phase of being 'top of the heap', and a change to Swindon ways on the LMS was just around the corner!

The Saga of the Scots

When in 1926 Sir Henry Fowler succeeded Hughes as chief mechanical engineer the Midland influence in design was supreme—small reliable locomotives, many compounds, and excellent detailed design.

The standard 4-4-0 compound was a first-class medium size locomotive. Several other Midland designs were also declared 'standard' by the LMS and did sterling work for years. However, the running department, which reigned supreme, urgently wanted a large express power locomotive for the West Coast Main Line. Fowler, who had started on the design of a large four-cylinder compound, was overtaken by events as when Anderson, the powerful motive power supremo, persuaded the management to bring over a GWR Castle class 4-6-0 to the LMS for tests. No. 5000 *Launceston Castle* did so well on the West Coast Main Line that the LMS board decided to go for a similar locomotive to meet the railway's needs. An exact copy was not available, partially for loading gauge reasons, so the North British Locomotive Company was commissioned to design and build a similar locomotive with three cylinders, in deference to Anderson's Derby training. The 4-6-0 design with a large boiler, high superheat and long-travel valve gear owed much to Midland details and Churchward ideas. A set of Lord Nelson drawings was also obtained from the Southern Railway, to give the basis for the firebox. Only one LNWR feature was incorporated, and a minor one at that. Fifty of these Royal Scots 4-6-0s were built by North British, starting in 1927. Twenty more were built at Derby, giving the LMS for the first time a modern reliable express design for the accelerated West Coast services.

Controversy has continued over the origins of this classic British locomotive design. E. S. Cox, who had a senior design position on the LMS, denied that it was a copy of the Lord Nelson 4-6-0s of the SR. Instead, he has pointed out the profusion of Midland details, including the cylinders, motion and main bearings. To the author's eye these had a distinctly 'Derby' look about them. The Royal Scots have been counted as one of the major successes of the steam era, with innumerable fast runs with heavy loads over Shap summit to their credit.

William Stanier

By 1931 the President of the LMS realised that he had to go outside to find the leadership in locomotive design needed to make his railway into a world leader. Apart from the Royal Scot 4-6-0s there were no locomotives among the 500 classes still running on the LMS that were capable of meeting the LNER challenge.

Sir Josiah Stamp feared that any of the lower officers of the mechanical engineer's department would steer closely to old design loyalties. He also realised that technological transfer only comes by transferring men; just sending drawings around from works to works will not do. So he went to the place where Churchward had worked out the basic way to build modern high speed but economical locomotives—Swindon— and he 'poached' one of that engineer's disciples, William Stanier, then fifty-five and happy in his work at Swindon.

The new man was a winner. From his Euston office a series of really great locomotive designs flowed out from 1932 to 1936. Although the first were the Princess Royal 4-6-2s, ex Midland lines saw much more of the Jubilees and the Black Fives, both six-coupled types. He had the ability to see the good in the existing LMS (mainly Midland) standard designs, coupled with the blessing of being able to spot his own mistakes. He quickly evolved two designs to meet this need grafting on the best of Midland detail to the best of Swindon practice, modified to meet the demands of the LMS water and coal supplies, more variable than the GW soft water and Welsh coal.

Black Fives and Jubilees

Of all the many fine designs to come off Stanier's drawing board, two had most impact on the Midland lines—'Black Fives' and Jubilees. A numerous class of taper boiler, two-cylinder 4-6-0s, the 'Black Fives' were mixed-traffic locomotives known as the 'driver's friend' and justly called ubiquitous by many a writer. The first 70 were built at Crewe and Vulcan Foundry with domeless boilers and a moderate degree of superheat. A success from the start, no fewer than 430 further locomotives were built by contractors and by LMS shops, the boiler steadily improved by enlarging the superheater area matched by a corresponding increase in firegrate area.

Their detailed mechanical design was particularly good, leading to a remarkably low rate of mechanical failure, representing only one hot box per locomotive per 15 years, with general repairs only necessary every 160,000 miles. Coal consumption was low at 3.13 lb/dbhp/hr in freight use, rising to 3.38 lb/dbhp/hr on express duties.

Capable of pulling long freight loads for hour after hour, the Class 5 4-6-0s were equally at home on express passenger work. O. S. Nock recorded twelve runs, two on the Midland routes, both first-class, topping 88 mph on the 'Main Line.' Even the severe S&D, with a massive load, gave a maximum of 68 mph. Not as spectacular as the great Pacifics designed by Stanier, they were, nevertheless an enduring reminder of his genius for economical, reliable engineering.

The Jubilees had a more complex provenance—'by Stanier, out of Baby Scot'. The taper boiler version of the Baby Scot—itself a Midlandised version of the LNWR Claughton—were not at first as successful as the Class 5s, suffering draughting problems. Soon after the first batch of 113 were in service, changes in blast orifice design, followed by boiler improvements, gave a reliable work machine, capable of spectacular performance, especially on the London—Nottingham runs. One train, the Manchester 10.15am down, required an average of 60mph St Pancras to Kettering, touching 85mph in places. This fine performance was reached day after day by the Jubilees, matched only by fine running over the punishing 'Peaks' line, through Miller's Dale and over Dove Holes summit.

Carriage and Wagon

Under LMS management Litchurch Lane became the principal carriage and wagon works, sharing some honours with Wolverton of the old LNWR. Soon Midland excellence came to the LMS with the prestige Royal Scot carriages turned out at Derby to the highest standards of Midland luxury. By 1930 the works was trusted with all the top orders for LMS rolling stock; the diners, buffet cars and kitchen cars built at Derby would have made Clayton proud. For

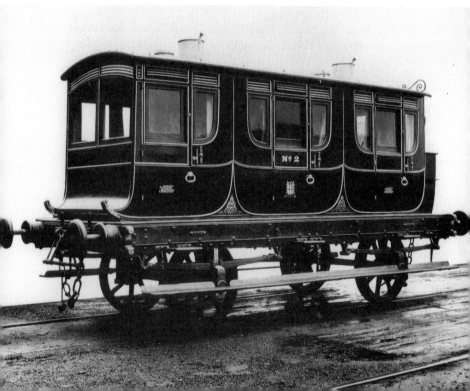

humbler duties over 1,000 general service coaches were turned out from the Derby shops, spreading right over the whole LMS system.

Timber bodies on steel underframes was the standard in the 1920s, with steel panels on timber framing gradually taking over from 1928. There was still a distinct Midland flavour in design and livery. Details of beading became progressively less fussy, but Midland designs were remarkably long lived, especially on the London, Tilbury & Southend coaches and the Glasgow suburbans, built between 1924 and 1935.

New ideas prevailed, with the gangwayed open and corridor coaches turned out on a production line basis to the tune of 1,211 thirds and 116 firsts between 1923 and 1939. Production methods had been modernised by the Works Manager R. W. Reid (later an LMS vice-president) who laid out a flow line from body lifting to painting shop. Mass production of wagons began in 1922, and soon the system was extended to include coaching stock and the repair of all LMS rolling stock. Brian Radford tells how during a single $5\frac{1}{2}$ day working week, the works produced 200 open wagons, 20 cattle wagons and 47 covered goods wagons. In the carriage building shop output of completed carriages was running at seven vehicles per week, the time taken for erecting the sides and ends of a coach being only 25 minutes, excluding the roof.

The LMS Midland

By 1930 the Midlandisation of the LMS was wearing off. Granet, Follows and Anderson had retired, and emphasis was switching to the

The Preserved 'half cab': This remarkable locomotive is now safe at the Midland Railway Trust site at Butterley. The sole preserved Midland tank engine now steams regularly, after much effort by the Trust. Designed by Johnson, it is an 0-6-0T, designated Class 1F. Ending its days at Staveley (Barrow Hill) shed, it continued service until 1965 when replaced by diesels. The oldest of a group stored at Rotherham, No 41708 was in reasonable condition, even though built in 1880 at a cost of only £1,600. Much loving work has now restored it to prime condition. *Midland Railway Trust.*

Stage coach on wheels: Photographed in 1933 at Derby Works, this Royal sleeping carriage of the early 1840s was built for Queen Adelaide, Dowager of King William IV, for use on the London & Birmingham Railway. Although not strictly a Midland coach, it was typical of the 'stage coach on wheels' design adopted by early railways. The coupé compartment was for the use of servants; the bulge at the far end was an extension for the royal feet when at rest! The carriage was at Derby Carriage & Wagon Works in the 1930s and now is at the National Railway Museum. *Derby Local Interest Library.*

Standard Clayton: This elegant Midland six-wheeler shows all the features of Clayton design. Built in 1874 by S. J. Clague & Co to Midland designs, it has the characteristic moulding around doors and windows, with M–R and class designation lettering at the waist. Note the arc roof used for much of the ordinary stock, despite the use of clerestory roofs in many express coaches. Some coaches of this type were fitted with Westinghouse brakes and labelled 'MSJS' for the joint Midland – Glasgow & South Western services to Glasgow and North British services to Edinburgh. *National Railway Museum.*

Midland LMS: The Midland heritage can be clearly seen in this fine Derby-built LMS lounge brake first. Apart from an unfussiness about the design, it is pure Clayton as developed by his successor Reid. *London Midland Region.*

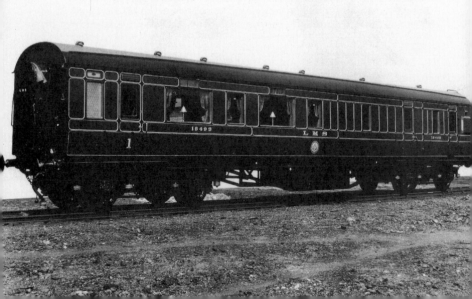

easier graded LNWR routes to Scotland and the North West. The great acceleration of LMS expresses in the 1930s benefited mainly the West Coast Main Line rather than the old Midland Settle & Carlisle to Carlisle and the Peak route to Manchester. Despite this, the operators were canny enough to realise that the scenic qualities of the Settle & Carlisle and the Peaks lines were considerable attractions. Traffic from the Midland towns to the North West and Scotland served to keep the old Midland services full. London to Midlands trains were as vigorous as their Midland precursors; some were even named on occasions, a most un-Derby-like idea!

The flagship of the inter-war St Pancras services was the Thames - Clyde Express, by 1939 a swift train from London to Glasgow via the old Midland lines and the 'Sou' West' route north of Carlisle. After a mile-a-minute sprint to Kettering, its pace slowed past Leicester and up the Erewash Valley, ignoring Derby and Nottingham, before taking the old NM line to Rotherham and on to Leeds and the high moors. Time to Glasgow was 8 hours 38 minutes, slow compared with the Mid Day Scot. Jubilees were the usual motive power, although Royal Scots were used for heavy wartime loadings, when this train was allowed ten hours with ten or more coaches.

The Thames-Clyde ran well into BR days, stopping at Nottingham and Sheffield, with a departure near to 10.00am, a useful time for an afternoon meeting in Sheffield or Leeds; it was known in the steel trade as the 'Gentleman's Train'. This pleasant train no longer runs. The down-grading of the S&C prior to possible closure left it without a route, so in 1974 the Thames-Clyde disappeared.

St Pancras to Manchester services have suffered a similar fate, with acceleration in the 1930s followed by closure in the 1960s. In 1938 two of the St Pancras to Lancashire trains were even named! The 10.30am was the Peak Express and the 4.30pm The Palatine. The Peak Express was part of a regular hourly Manchester service from St Pancras, but it was smartly timed at 3 hours 35 minutes. Motive power was usually a Jubilee, although for a time a Class 5 was put on at Derby to accommodate a tight loading gauge. Post-war, this train took the load while the WCML was electrified. Diesel-hauled, the train was a sell-out until the old LNWR route to Manchester was reopened, with its 100mph expresses. The Peak route then quickly disappeared.

One innovation of the LMS was the regular Manchester to Bournemouth through trains, made popular by the increase of paid holidays between the wars. The renowned Pines Express left Manchester at 10.10am, taking LNWR metals to New Street where it entered Midland territory, as far as Bath, Queen Square (later Green Park).

Reversing onto the S&D line it ran to Broadstone, when a few miles of Southern Railway brought the Pines Express journey's end at Bournemouth West. The journey time of 6 hours 27 minutes was not scorching. This was increased in BR days, with the added indignity of ancient Midland clerestory stock! Nevertheless, the 'Pines' was a grand train in its day, taking thousands of Lancastrians to the seaside at a speed completely acceptable in a more leisurely age.

Pride of place on the LMS Midland main line went to the Nottingham trains. For many years there was a popular up service from Nottingham to St Pancras at around 8.00am. Timings of 140 minutes for the 123 miles of the Melton route were common, with coaches slipped at Kettering, then a junction for Cambridge. By 1939 times were close to the two hours until the war intervened.

No amount of preference for Euston services by the LMS management was allowed to interfere with the speed and usefulness of the Sheffield, Nottingham and Leicester services. The LNER had introduced The Master Cutler, a crack early-morning express on old GC metals, stealing most of the Sheffield morning business traffic from the LMS, but Sheffield was always a 'Midland' preserve and the LMS successfully fought off LNER competition until after World War II. In March 1925 a return St Pancras-Sheffield-Bradford service left Sheffield at 9.55am reaching London in around the three hours. This train was joined by a second daily fast service to catch the London to Sheffield business trade. Post-war, The Master Cutler still took the London-bound early-morning traffic, but for the Sheffield-bound traveller St Pancras was the best station to use.

Through trains from Yorkshire to the West of England continued to flourish in LMS days, one being The Devonian. This Bradford to Bristol train carried three coaches for Torquay, leaving Bradford (Forster Square) at 10.52am and Sheffield at 11.42 reaching Bristol via the old B&G line.

Late Improvements

By 1933 the LMS had enough confidence and government support to carry out some badly needed improvements. The line from Derby to Ambergate was chronically overcrowded. Manchester and Leeds expresses rubbed shoulders with a procession of coal and mineral trains on the two tracks north of Duffield. Two tracks were added as far as Ambergate, where the Peak line diverged from the old North Midland. This short but expensive quadrupling meant four tracks were available from London to Ambergate Junction, one pair taking the Melton route, the other through Leicester.

General goods continued much as in MR times—a network of stopping goods trains, serving all but the smallest country station, each taking a lot of time, shunting off 10-ton wagons, picking up others at each wayside stop. Road transport of goods was still rare and the railway had most of this infinitely varied traffic.

On the mineral side, the 1930s saw an expansion in iron-ore carriage to the vast new Corby steel plant, built on the Melton line, a few miles north of Kettering. Coal and limestone were also needed by the voracious furnaces, while the products of the works gave much trade to the ex-Midland main line. Corby continued to give work to the railway throughout the remaining life of the LMS, declining only in BR times. Further north, the great iron works at Stanton Park prospered as war approached. In Sheffield an amalgamation of steel firms into the United Steel Companies ensured that the old MR tracks around Attercliffe, Rotherham and the Nunnery were kept busy with mineral wagons and flat trucks taking away the long products of the mills.

When trolleybus competition hit other London suburban inner-ring railways in the 1930s, the damage to the old Midland 'inner' services had already been done, with the closure of Haverstock Hill and Welsh Harp before 1923.

On the goods front the Midland shared the misery of the great depression, when UK goods haulage fell from 507 million tons in 1907 to 239 million tons in 1932. One saviour was the vast growth of London between the wars, when thousands of semi-detached houses were built in areas served by the myriad of MR coal depots. Hendon, Golders Green, Finchley and a host of other dormitory towns, with street upon street of new building, ensured that the Toton to Cricklewood coal traffic increased steadily. This had been usually double-headed by Class 4 0-6-0s, but with increasing pressure on line occupation a really big puller was needed. After abortive trials with the Lickey Banker 0-10-0, Derby ordered three 2-6-0+0-6-2 Beyer-Garratts. This batch had standard Midland bearings, and were always in the railway works with hot axle boxes. A further batch was more successful, being allocated to Toton and Wellingborough for the London coal traffic. Unpopular with firemen, they used over 130 lb of coal a mile, and had 14 sand boxes which needed filling before each trip. The massive rotary hopper tenders did nothing to help the poor fireman shovel the coal into the firebox and blisters were the order of the day on a Garratt turn.

Map of the Midland Railway lines in the Nottinghamshire coalfield

Local LMS services continued in Midland fashion with intense services in the Notts-Derbyshire coal areas, in and around Birmingham, and north of Sheffield. Stopping trains pulled by tireless 'Jinty' 0-6-0Ts worked up the Erewash Valley from Nottingham, through Trent, stopping at all stations to Chesterfield. The first train of the day at 6.12am from Nottingham took two hours to Chesterfield, unacceptable today, but vital in the 1930s before widespread car ownership. Other stoppers ran to Mansfield, with connecting locals between Pye Bridge and Ambergate along the little branch to Ilkeston and between Pye Bridge and Westhouses. These trains took miners to work, children to school, mothers shopping, regular as clockwork with clean, red carriages and friendly staff.

The LMS continued the useful South Birmingham locals, running down to Redditch via King's Norton, or to King's Norton via Camp Hill. Redditch was also served by the Ashchurch via Evesham route, completing the raft of Birmingham locals.

The LMS ran the 'Bed-Pan' service from London to Bedford, with a useful set of slow trains mixed in with semi-fasts for the growing traffic from the St Albans area. While these services prospered, continuing into BR days and electrification, the orbital line through South Tottenham, Barking and Southend withered under a policy of neglect, but survives today.

By 1938 the time had come to accelerate the Midland Division services. Leicester could now be reached in an average of 104 minutes by 23 trains daily, Nottingham in 138 minutes by 18 trains, and Sheffield in 188 minutes by 19 daily trains. The 1938 Sheffield timings have hardly changed today. That year also saw a big improvement in freight handling when Toton sidings were modernised. The down yard was brought up-to-scratch in 1939, the up yard's facelift took until 1952, delayed by World War II. The down yard handled 5,000 wagons a day, while the up yard was by 1952 completely reconstructed into 37 roads, plus 11 arrival roads and 20 storage roads. In its hey-day in the 1950s, Toton handled two million wagons a year.

10

THE MIDLAND TODAY

High Speed to the Midlands

The Midland is alive and well and serves the Midlands towns by high-speed train. In the post-Beeching state of the old Midland Railway a regular service of HSTs leaves St Pancras for Wellingborough, Kettering, Leicester and points north. Kettering is less than an hour from London, attracting commuters, while Leicester is but 15 minutes over the hour by clean comfortable trains, claiming an extra 40 per cent of passengers on HST introduction in 1983. Alternate services split after Lougborough, one to Nottingham, the other an hour later going north via Derby to Sheffield, reached in $2\frac{1}{2}$ hours, slowed by the need to divert from the Erewash Valley line to call at Derby or Nottingham. The Midland Main line services are very fast, those to Leicester ranking fourth in the UK speed table. Soon to have colour signalling, BR is putting a lot of money into the London-Nottingham-Derby line, up-rating many of the stations and improving amenities.

The other old Midland main line, Yorkshire to the West of England, also thrives; nine HSTs a day go from the North-East to Cardiff or Bristol, some starting from Newcastle. Cardiff to Birmingham is a two-hour journey, easily beating the time by road, while Cardiff to Derby is well under three hours, the time to Newcastle is five-and-a-half, unattainable by car. There are good cross-platform connections at New Street for Manchester and Glasgow, making cross-country train travel far easier than the delights of the M6 and M1 combination.

In the London area, the line to Bedford is electrified, the one-man-operated 25kV trains running a frequent service to St Pancras and Moorgate via the Metropolitan Widened Lines. When the 'Bed-Pan' service started, the track to Sharnbrook had been re-signalled, a new platform added at Luton, and Bedford rebuilt just north of the old MR station. This service, which has revitalised stations south of

Bedford, was to be extended in May 1988 south of the Thames with the re-opening of the former SECR Snow Hill Tunnel near St Paul's, connecting the City Widened Lines once more to the Southern network. Dual 25kV ac and 750V dc trains are used for cross-river services, cutting out the cross-London inter-station journey for north-south passengers. Channel Tunnel connections also loom in the planners' minds.

Birmingham commuter services, never too bright, were revived when Cross-City was made out of the old LNWR line to Lichfield and the Midland loop down to King's Norton and Redditch via Selly Oak. The LNWR portion was largely unchanged, but the Midland leg benefited from new stations at Five Ways, University and Longbridge. Cross-City passenger services are boosted by the growth of the new town at Redditch and by the excellence of the rebuilt New Street Station, right in the heart of the Birmingham shopping area.

Modest development of the old Midland line north of Leeds, led by the local passenger transport authority, has allowed Saltair and Cross-flats stations to be re-opened. Otherwise, the Midland lines in the Leeds area have declined somewhat, with Bradford services taking a knock when the new Bradford station was sited on GN territory.

The old Midland line between Sheffield and Leeds has suffered varied fates in recent years and is now used by Leeds to Sheffield trains over only part of its length. Services were diverted between Moorthorpe and Wakefield Westgate until 1973, when they reverted to the old Midland main line, with a few trains serving Westgate by means of a tortuous diversion. Now the through Leeds-Sheffield trains use the MR line only south of Dearne Junction, at first passing the poorly-sited Rotherham (Masborough) station on their way to Sheffield. Rotherham is better served now the new Holmes link is open, enabling trains to reach the old GC station, much nearer to the city centre than Masborough

True, there have been closures, only post-Hudson lines in the main, as the old rogue knew a good line when he saw one. Even the cross-country Nottingham to Lincoln and the Leicester to Peterborough remain. The books in the *Forgotten Railways* series are amazingly quiet about the old Midland!

There have been some closures since the end of World War II. The Bath and Bristol connections have given way to the GWR routes and the Swansea Valley Midland connection has gone. The branches to Thornbury, Dursley and Nailsworth have joined the rural peace of the Redditch and Ashchurch loop and the MR Malvern line in the Midlands. Bedford to Hitchin and to Northampton disappeared along with the crawling Huntingdon line, while the Melton loop is now goods-only apart from the Hudson-built section in the middle. Further north, the Peak route was cut at Matlock when the WCML was electrified, losing a useful safety valve. Eastward in Nottinghamshire, Mansfield is the largest town in the UK not on BR, fobbed-off with the indignity of a Parkway station miles across the valley. Despite these cuts the Buxton branch survives for the considerable stone traffic from the limestone quarries, finding the old LNWR line too steep for the heavy mineral trains.

This said though, the old Midland lines survive amazingly well. Not so their erstwhile competitors—the GN routes into Nottinghamshire and Derbyshire have been decimated, the LNW branches through Northamptonshire have gone, and the Great Central is no more. Sheffield is a 'Midland' town again as Sheffield Victoria, built by the MS&L gathers dust along with the MS&L route across the Pennines, while the MR Manchester line through Totley thrives.

Stations

Fortunately St Pancras remains as ever, a grand station building with a gentlemanly air, providing fast services to the Shires. Easily the most pleasant of the London termini, without the chaos of Liverpool Street or the frantic rush of London Bridge, St Pancras survives despite several efforts to run its trains into overcrowded King's Cross. The baronial booking hall was saved from destruction by the combined efforts of the Victorian Society and an enlightened Secretary of State. Apart from the 'Gentlemen's Hall', all else is pleasing, with convenient refreshment facilities and a bright bookstall. Departures are never rushed, but then they never were. Barlow's great roof, repainted and well-lit, presides over well-patronised, frequent HST 125s to the Midlands, interspersed with 'Bed-Pan' services spilling commuters into the London Underground. The only thing that mars this elegance is the inadequate Underground entrance, London Underground Ltd at its Dickensian worst. Soon, long-awaited improvements will reduce the gales that rush through summer and winter, when a screen is erected to weatherproof the Euston Road.

The long redundant Somers Town goods depot will soon arise anew, rebuilt as the British Library, standing beside St Pancras, the apt memorial to the heroes of the Midland—Ellis, Allport and Barlow.

After years of neglect, BR has turned its attention to other fine

Midland main line station stations. True, Leicester has been well refurbished for some time, but now BR is carying out a major over-haul at Nottingham Midland and at Derby. Judging by Leicester, these will become comfortable and well-appointed stations, with re-freshment facilities as bright and clean as the new main buffet at Sheffield Midland. In the north, Leeds City is an excellent replace-ment for the ramshackle Wellington. Rotherham will benefit from the new Holmes link, taking trains nearer to the city centre. In the south the outer suburban stations—all remaining today—are clean and well-tended. The only note of sadness is the complete rebuilding of the old Derby station frontage, despite the fashion for recasting new wine into elegant old bottles. Oh that BR could have kept the *porte cochère*—after all, it did rebuild Wellingborough keeping the barge-boarded main building intact.

Goods Services

These too have changed, more than passenger trains. Gone are the stopping goods, pulled by an ancient 0-6-0 and shunting at every wayside station. Gone are the long London coal trains pulled down the main line by a Beyer-Garratt at 20mph from Toton to Cricklewood. London now uses gas or oil for heating its houses, while most goods are delivered to shops by truck. The 0-6-0s and the Garratts have been replaced by fast fitted rakes of container flats speeding between a few Speed Link computer-controlled concentration depots. Toton is one of this select band, its big yards still busy day and night with container loads instead of old-fashioned 10-ton wagons. Coal still trundles along MR tracks but in vast merry-go-round trains from the Nottingham-shire pits to the Trent Valley power stations. Mineral traffic also thrives, mainly for stone now that the Northamptonshire iron-ore mines are no longer economical, and steel is made with foreign ore brought to Port Talbot or Hunterston in 100,000 ton carriers. Stone for road-making now fills special trains (to BR's profit), at Barrow and Quorn, near Loughborough. Limestone still goes by the old Midland metals from Buxton and from the Swinden Quarry, keeping the Skipton-Grassington branch largely intact. Aggregate also goes from this quarry down to Leeds in a fleet of special air-braked hopper wagons, in 1,100 ton capacity rakes.

Derby Today

Derby remains very much at the centre of technical excellence of British railway engineering—British Rail has established its Tech-

185

nical Centre at Derby, responsible for the design of a host of modern rail concepts including the High-Speed Train and the Advanced Passenger Train. Newly built, just across the road from the 'Carriage and Wagon' in Litchurch lane, the Technical Centre is a world beater.

Now part of British Rail Engineering Ltd., the carriage and wagon works prospers and can be justly thought of as the flagship of BREL. The Mark III coach was designed and built for BR at Litchurch Lane, one of the world's most comfortable and safe passenger coaches and the foundation of the successful HST sets. This concept has been extended at Derby into the 'international coach', adapting easily to any loading gauge, and made by production-line methods to give a flexible, economical design to the highest standards of comfort for operators world-wide. Derby maintenance experience has been used to keep running costs as low as possible while keeping comfort at Midland levels in the Clayton tradition. The first ten 'Internationals' went to the Gabon in 1984. Another Derby-designed international winner is the railbus. A low-cost version of the BR diesel multiple-unit, this road coach put on a rail chassis has toured the Far East on an impressive demonstration tour. A demonstration model for the North American market is more luxurious, with air-conditioning and real Derby furnishings for a more sophisticated market. The European version more closely matches the rail buses in Northern Ireland.

Midland Steam

Although not attracting so much interest from the steam preservation movement as the old GWR lines, steam-hauled trains can still be seen on Midland metals, hauled by Midland locomotives. Within sight of the Butterley works, home of the St Pancras roof, the Midland Railway Trust runs a regular steam train passenger service on part of the Ambergate to Pye Bridge line. The trust is also the focal point of a major industrial museum project planned to show many aspects of the Midland in its glory.

Three-and-a-half miles of track are used for the trains, starting from a station at Butterley, reconstructed from the old Midland station building at Whitwell. The museum, under construction at Swanwick Junction will be of major importance to students of pre-Grouping lines. The Trust has a Kirtley Class 156 locomotive, built in 1866 and withdrawn in 1947. Of equal interest is the half cab 0-6-0T No 41708, one of the useful Class 1F employed on shunting and light passenger duties on the Midland. Those locomotives were seen on passenger workings on the Hemel Hempstead branch, and on the rural line to Dursley as late as 1957, No 41708, turned out from Derby works in 1880, is now in full working order again and regularly pulls passenger trains on the Trust's layout, a fine example of the 'living museum' approach at Butterley.

Further north, just off the old main line, the Worth Valley was opened in 1867 from Keighley to Oxenholme, north-west of Leeds. Closed in 1961 as uneconomic, one of the earliest preservation societies brought steam back to the Worth Valley in 1968 after eight years' effort. The line is well stocked with working locomotives including one Midland Class 4 0-6-0. The stations are all authentic Midland-built to last, no frills, and excellent for their purpose. Oakworth, seen in detail in the film *The Railway Children*, is restored in every detail, fire in the grate, curious advertisements and, (so the author is told) an authentic ladies retiring room. This scenic and pleasant line is an asset to the holidaymaker and fascinating to the steam enthusiast.

Further north again, the Settle to Carlisle is used for the popular steam-hauled Cumbrian Mountain Express, running between Leeds and Carlisle. Although bereft of real Midland motive power, the 'long drag' gives a challenge to the mighty locomotives—Jubilee 4-6-0 No 5690 *Leander*, Princess Royal 4-6-2 No 6201 *Princess Elizabeth*, and Coronation Class 8P 4-6-2 No 6229 *Duchess of Hamilton* from LMS days. Long may the S&C live!

BIBLIOGRAPHY

General

The Midland Railway was most fortunate with its first historian, Frederick Williams. The present author hopes that any reader interested in delving deeper into the fascinating saga of the Midland will be able to beg, borrow or otherwise acquire a copy of *The Midland Railway—Its Rise and Progress*, published just as the Settle to Carlisle line was opening. This superb book takes us from the beginning of the Midland's precursor lines right up to the construction of the S&C in well-written detail, enlivened with beautiful engravings, missing only those incidents which put in a poor light characters alive in 1876.

Two other books tell the story of the Midland up to 1923, each excellent in its own way, but now out of print. The two-volume history by E. G. Barnes, *The Rise of the Midland Railway* and *The Midland Main Line* concentrates on the growth of the system, on its organisational and managerial structure, somewhat neglecting the locomotive side. In contrast Hamilton Ellis' *The Midland Railway* speeds through the build-up of the system, but is full of fascinating accounts of locomotive development and operation.

Early Days

Three fascinating books describe the Midland's precursor lines in detail. Clinker's *The Leicester & Swannington Railway* and Whishaw's *The Railways of Great Britain and Ireland* tell the story of the early lines in their own ways. Clinker's short book is a model of railway history, while Francis Whishaw, a civil engineer writing in the 1840s, describes the main lines open by 1845 in detail, even to the type of track and make of rolling stock. Luckily 'Whishaw' has been reprinted and is well worth a read. George Hudson's life was so bound up in the early days of the Midland that *The Railway King* by Richard Lambert is full of atmosphere as well as good historical details of the Midland's formative years. As the early years of the railways were also bound up with the still thriving canal system, Charles Hadfield's *Canals of the East Midlands* will prove to be a valuable companion to the railway histories. The stagecoach drivers were accustomed to give a running historical and economic commenting to their journeys; early rail travellers made do with small books known as *Companions* giving full details of even the smallest village traversed by the line. The *Notts and Derby Railway Companion*, published in 1839 (and reprinted as document No. 3 of the Derby Record Society) served this function for the Derby to Nottingham line of the Midland Counties, adding information about connections to London via Rugby, and to Birmingham and Manchester. The advertisements in the *Companion* are a joy to the 1980s reader.

Some volumes of the *Victoria History of the Counties of England* give good accounts of early railway development. Notable are those on Leicestershire and Warwickshire, whose editors, fortunately, placed railway history well to the fore and have excellent mini-histories of the railways near Birmingham and near Leicester respectively.

Locomotives and Carriages

Midland locomotives have been less well described than those of the GWR, but some books shed light on the profound effect Kirtley and Johnson had on locomotive development in the Nineteenth Century. E. L. Ahrons' *The British Steam Locomotive* contains a host of references to the Kirtley and Johnson days at Derby. Fortunately, Johnson, who was a world class mechanical engineer, was also President of the Institution of Mechanical Engineers in 1898. His Presidential Address is a cornucopia of knowledge about his lines' locomotives and their performance.

Locomotive enthusiasts will also gain much pleasure from Brian Radford's *Derby Works and Midland Locomotives*, but will need a copy of the *British Locomotive Catalogue* Volume 3A to unravel the tortuous numbering schemes of successive Midland locomotive managers. We are also fortunate in having E. S. Cox's *Locomotive Panorama* to tell us of the amazing corporate infighting at Derby during the early years of the LMS, when Midlandisation was all the rage.

The Midland carriage is rightly documented in detail in a superbly illustrated book by Dow and Lacy, a work of meticulous detail written from a basis of detailed knowledge and understanding of Midland Railway History.

Stations

Midland Stations have also received a good press, starting with Barlow's own account of his designs for St Pancras in the *Proceedings* of the Institution of Civil Engineers, Volume 30. St Pancras is also the topic of a book to itself, by the doyen of railway historians, Jack Simmons. The majority of Midland stations are pictured in *Midland Line Memories* by Brian Radford and in *Midland Railway Architecture* by Andersen and Fox. A detailed description of general Midland style in every item from stations to lamp posts and signals is given in *Midland Style* by the Historical Railway Model Society. The widely ranging *Victorian Stations* by Biddle is a good general account, covering all railways in Great Britain, with a host of references to Midland stations.

Settle & Carlisle

The Settle & Carlisle has suffered from a surfeit of words flowing from the pens of innumerable authors. Two books on the S&C can be particularly recommended: *The Story of the Settle-Carlisle Line* by Houghton and Forster, and for a description of the endurance of the navvies and their families living on the moors in the fierce Westmorland winters *The Railway Shanties* by W. R. Mitchell.

General Background

Several 'how it was' books have been written about railway life on former Midland lines in the 1930s. One, describing the busy life of a small country station, is *Recollections of Country Station Life* by Harry Alland. Another, *Wellingborough Memories* deals with the life of a locomotive man on the Toton to Cricklewood coal runs, Beyer Garratts and all. Those interested in country railway life should not miss *The Country Railway* by David St John Thomas.

Much can also be learned form the *Regional History* series, especially:

Volume 7   West Midlands   Rex Christiansen

Volume 8	East Midlands	Robin Leleux
Volume 9	South and West Yorkshire	David Joy
Volume 13	The Lake Counties	David Joy

Strangely enough the series on *Forgotten Railways* is not too informative about the M.R. as so much of the old system still remains. However, the volume on East Midlands by J. H. Anderson gives a detailed history of the old Notts and Derby coal lines.

Students of the Midland should also not be without *Red for Danger* by L. T. C. Rolt for a vivid and accurate account of the accidents on the line in the late 19th and early 20th Centuries.

The first of the three-volume general description of the development of the British railway system by Jack Simmons is a 'must' for all lovers of the Midland system and its development. Equally essential to the Midland student is Volume 2 of *Locomotive and Train working in the late Nineteenth Century* by A. L. Ahrons, an idiosyncratic Nottingham engineer, trained at Swindon, who travelled widely and wrote penetrating accounts of railway operations, full of 'atmosphere' as well as details of train workings and locomotive performances.

The Railway Navvies by Coleman and *The Railway Age* by Robbins can be read with profit to round off the general picture of the world of the pre-Grouping lines. Those fortunate enough to have access to copies of *The Railway Magazine* from the early years of this century will find a host of references to the Midland—1904 was a particularly rich year, full of 'pushes' by our expanding railway, looking for business. One last bibliographic note—no serious student of the Midland should be without a copy of the *Bibliography of Railway History* by Ottley!